NEW KIDS ON THE BLOCK

JOSEPH, JONATHAN, DONNIE, DANNY, and JORDAN

OUR STORY

BANTAM BOOKS

NEW YORK · TORONTO · LONDON · SYDNEY · AUCKLAND

This book is dedicated to the ones we love—our families, friends, and most especially, our fans.

Our sincere thanks go to each and every person who helped get this project off the ground and into a book we are proud of— you've all got The Right Stuff!

OUR STORY: NEW KIDS ON THE BLOCK

A Bantam Book/July 1990

Front cover photograph copyright © 1990 by Todd Kaplan
Back cover photographs copyright © 1990 by Larry Busacca
DESIGN BY BETH TONDREAU DESIGN/MARY A. WIRTH

Library of Congress Card Number: 90–619

ISBN 0-553-34872-8

Published simultaneously in the United States and Canada

Bantam Books are published by Bantam Books, a division of Bantam Doubleday Dell Publishing Group, Inc. Its trademark, consisting of the words "Bantam Books" and the portrayal of a rooster, is Registered in U.S. Patent and Trademark Office and in other countries. Marca Registrada. Bantam Books, 666 Fifth Avenue, New York, New York 10103.

PRINTED IN THE UNITED STATES OF AMERICA

W   10 9 8 7 6 5 4 3 2 1

All photos in color section are © 1989, 1990 by Larry Busacca with the exception of photos on pages 12 (bottom), 14 (© 1990 Todd Kaplan), 13 (© 1988 Elizabeth Marshall).

CONTENTS

PART I: KIDSTUFF

PART II: MUSICALSTUFF

PART III: PERSONALSTUFF

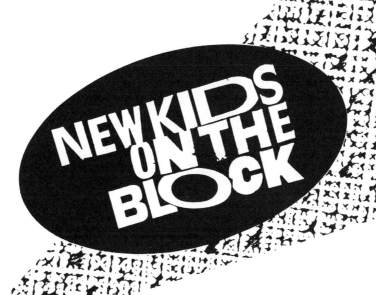

NEW KIDS ON THE BLOCK

DONNIE
WAHLBERG

BEGINNING AT THE BEGINNING...

I was born in 1969, August 17. You know what's funny, I used to be excited that I was born in 1969, 'cause it was a great year. So many great things happened. It's kinda scary to think that someone might say one day, "Yeah, that was the year Donnie Wahlberg was born." *That's crazy!*

I've been in Boston my whole life, my whole family's been in Boston their whole lives. I've never lived outside of Dorchester—which is a section of Boston—in my life, 'till just now.

When I was born, I was the eighth, but my little brother Mark, the youngest, he's the ninth. I've got an older brother Bobbo, then next older, there's Tracey, then Jimbo, Paul, Michelle, Arthur, and Debbie's the oldest. Don't ask me ages, because I don't know anyone in my family's ages. My parents are Alma and Donald. My full name is Donald E. Wahlberg, Jr. My mother always called me Baby Donnie. My friends called me Donnie, only in school was I

called Donald. Donnie was always spelled the same way. When I was real little, my dad got me a baseball shirt with my name on it. That's how it was spelled and that's how I like it.

When I was born, we lived in an apartment in Dorchester. We bought a house when I was about five years old. My brothers Arthur and Paul shared a room, my three sisters were together and four of us younger boys were in the same room. We had all bunk beds, but sometimes I'd go share with Mark. I always liked the feeling of having lots of other kids in the room with me—to this day, I don't like being alone.

My father was kinda strict, stricter than my mother. It wasn't that my parents didn't allow us to do things, they were good. I mean, some of my friends couldn't even go up to certain neighborhoods, things like that. My family was never worried about that. I could do anything I wanted during the course of the day, as long as I was back for dinner. They didn't have many rules, but the ones they did, they liked to enforce. I never got grounded or anything like that, but if I did something messed up, they'd make me stay in, just for that night, or something. And that would be torture enough, because I wanted to always be out, runnin' the streets and stuff.

I know that my parents sometimes feel that they didn't do a good job, and I always try and tell them that they did a *great* job. One of my brothers, Jimbo, he really had problems growin' up. He even spent some time in jail. But now that we look back on it, we kind of realize that Jimbo and I, we both grew up in the same house, had the same upbringing, same advantages and disadvantages—and made completely different choices about things. Jimbo's decisions got him into trouble. Maybe seeing him go down made me stay positive even though he did wild stuff he always influenced me to do good. I'm not ashamed of him and I hope he isn't ashamed of himself. Every day I see him living straight, it makes me proud to be a Wahlberg.

We had the usual brotherly rivalries in my family. Like we'd fight over who was the best looking, who had the best build, who was the toughest, stuff like that. We'd roughhouse, throw pillows, wrestle. But that was among us. Forget it if someone outside the family tried to mess with one of us—he'd have to take *all* of us on.

When I was growing up, I was always the family peacemaker. I couldn't stand to see people fighting—not seriously fighting, that is—I would always try to convince whoever was fighting to make up. Even now, I can't leave the house mad at somebody, I can't go to bed mad, I can't hang up the phone if I'm still arguing. There's something in me, I don't know what it is, but it's like I just have to fix things. Can't leave them unresolved. It hurts too much.

When things started goin' right for one of us, things started goin' right for everyone. When I started gettin' the records goin' and stuff, all of a sudden I noticed that my brother was gettin' out of jail and my other brother finally became a carpenter, which he'd been trying to do for years. And my other brother got a job on a cruise ship as a chef, which was his big thing. And my sister got married and had a baby and they're all doin' great. I'm proud of my family, and proud of my parents, it's funny when you are not with your family for a while you really start to realize how much we all take our families for granted. It may not seem like a big deal to be able to walk through the house in your underwear with your sister around, but live in a hotel room for 2 years and you'll see how really special and close a family is. My family is truly where my heart is. I love them. I miss them, but also I enjoy sharing my success with them. They're like celebrities too now. I love sharing my good fortune with them. There's so many things I wanted when I had no money. Now I don't want them. I just want to do for my friends and family. Money, fame, status—that don't mean Jack to me if I ain't got my family here cuz if you think about it a family is all you've got.

HARD LESSONS

We didn't have a lot in those days, but I didn't feel poor, because I didn't really reach for more than I could get. My mom always worked, first at a bank and then at a hospital, because we needed two incomes. My dad drove a truck for a while and then a bus, delivering school lunches and in the summers, camp lunches. I guess we were poor, but we always had plenty to eat, big dinners every night and really big meals on Sunday nights.

We knew we had more than a lot of other people. When my father was delivering the school lunches, he used to bring all the extras home. See, sometimes there were extra lunches that didn't get eaten and the schools were going to trash them. But my father felt, no, this is good food, it shouldn't go to waste. So he'd bring them home, break them all down and we'd go around the neighborhood, delivering them to kids all over. And if we knew that a family was really needy, we'd give them lots of extra special stuff. And my friends thought it was cool, y'know, that we had all this school lunch stuff. They'd come over and say, "Oh, Donnie, could I get a package of cookies and a chocolate milk?"

The one time it was the hardest for us was when the school bus company that my dad worked for went on strike. We really had no money. But my father stuck by the union and I'm glad he did what he did. You know, people were telling him, "Go back to work." But my dad was a strong union man and he stood up for what he believed in. And that

TOP:
My brother Arthur, 1989 (© 1989 Larry Busacca)

MIDDLE:
With brother Mark in Maine (courtesy Alma Conroy)

BOTTOM:
Me, Bobbo and Mark as teenagers (courtesy Alma Conroy)

helped me learn to stand up for what I believe in. He even lost one of his best friends who crossed the picket line.

When his company was on strike, we really had no money and we got food stamps. For a while, I never thought about it, but I remember one day I was going to the store with one of my brothers and my friend. And this friend, he was like a real peer to my brother, he hung with my brother's crowd. And I wanted to get milk and Pepsi. And I said, "I got a dollar and a food stamp," and my brother slapped me. And I didn't understand, I was like, "Why did you do that? What's wrong?" Before, I didn't worry about admitting stuff like that, but because he worried about it, it made me worry about it too. It was dumb to be ashamed of that, but it's part of growing up. Our society makes us ashamed to be poor, ashamed to have pimples, ashamed to be ourselves, but I want my fans to never be ashamed of who they are—no matter how bad things seem to be they have to stay proud and stay strong. Life is too short to worry about wrinkles in your jeans. When people shout you down, you must know they are only trying to find strength in your so-called "weaknesses" because they themselves are weak. I hope someday the world won't be like this. People won't judge other people cuz they're different or whatever but if we keep a positive attitude now and teach it to our kids and the next generation, then maybe someday America will finally live up to its reputation and truly become the land of the free.

Another thing about when I was young—my parents would do some things for us that they felt were important. They might not have given us money to go to the movies, or do this and that, but when baseball season came around, if we wanted to play they would really try and get that money together so we could. And they struggled to pay for my sister's dance lessons.

THINGS WE DID TOGETHER

We used to have these family bingo games every week. And my dad would be the caller, call out the numbers. And I would take it so seriously—I always wanted to win. I hated to lose and really got upset if I lost. I'd bribe people to change cards with me, so I'd have a better chance of winning but I always used card #3. It was fun, we laughed a lot. My grandmother always won.

My mom used to take us a lot of places, not just us, but other kids in the neighborhood too. In December, she'd take everyone to go see Santa Claus. In the summers, on her days off, she'd take us all to the beach. We'd get there really early, like eight in the morning and stay all day. And then at night, she'd take us to drive-in movies. Sometimes on

T O P :
My and mom, 1989 (courtesy Alma Conroy)

M I D D L E :
My stepdad Mark and my dog Sandy (courtesy Alma Conroy)

B O T T O M :
My sister Tracey the dancer (courtesy Alma Conroy)

O P P O S I T E   L E F T :
(© 1990 Todd Kaplan)

O P P O S I T E   R I G H T :
My family on Christmas morning (courtesy Alma Conroy)

Friday nights, we'd all pile in her bed and watch TV—only we'd usually all fall asleep right away! Those times were special cuz my mom worked so hard but all her time off she spent with us.

Halloweens were real cool at our house, my parents always made a big deal of it. We had a playroom in the basement and they'd make it like a spook house. They'd get dressed up as skeletons or ghosts and try to scare us. We'd always have parties down there, every Halloween, bobbing for apples and stuff like that. Two years in a row, me and Mark got dressed up like ballerinas, in tutus—it was hysterical.

Christmas was our best time as a family. See, it was the most important, special day of the year to my parents and they'd save all the rest of the year to make it wonderful for us. Like they'd spend all this money on presents for us—you couldn't even walk in our house, for all the presents around. I think for a while they made me really believe in Santa Claus cuz they didn't make a lot of money, but on Christmas there'd be many presents for all nine of us! That shows how dedicated they were to us.

And my best memory is of Christmas morning. We'd all wake up, all nine of us, like at four in the morning or something, and sit, lined up on the steps, waiting for our parents to wake up. We wouldn't go downstairs to that tree, with all those presents underneath, until they woke up. I don't know why we were so good—but we were. As soon as they did wake up though, we'd all go tearing down the steps and dive into our presents. One year, I'll never forget, there were nine bikes around the tree.

> **I always hated people who tried to do things just to look cool. And I did it too. I smoked just to be a cool guy... I never got into the habit of smoking, it was just something I did to try and be cool...But when I met the Kool Aid Bunch, I wasn't worried about being cool anymore.**

But presents weren't the real reason Christmas was the most special. It was more the warm, loving feelings that we all had for each other. My mother made such a beautiful tree and the house would be lit so nice. It would be snowing and she always played her Johnny Mathis Christmas tape. Man, I would feel so Christmasy it was beautiful.

WHAT I WAS LIKE

Everyone has this impression of me as this wild kid, but actually I was a lot more quiet when I was little. I was shy. I remember being real shy, like it took a lot for me to go up and talk to people and stuff.

I think I was crazy, too, when I was real young, but I picked my spots. When I wasn't being shy, I was being crazy. A lot of older people always liked me when I was little. All the teachers always seemed to like me. My whole life I've been able to get along with adults.

I was a funny kid, I used to always tell jokes. I liked to be the center of attention, but I don't know why that was. Because I was still shy, y'know, and I was self-conscious, so maybe I wanted to be the center of attention and be, like, successful at being the center of attention.

When I got to know people, I was always real outgoing. If I was running with the crowd and a new kid came along, I always wanted to make him a part of our crowd. I'm very sensitive . . . very sensitive . . . probably too sensitive.

SCHOOL DAYS

I went to kindergarten by my house, but after that, I went on the bus to the William Monroe Trotter School in the next neighborhood over, which was Roxbury.

A few of my brothers and sisters—Jimbo, Bobbo, Tracey went to the Trotter School before me, so I didn't think about it, about being bused to school. That's the way it was. It wasn't as if I had walked to a neighborhood school for four years and suddenly got bused to another one—being bused was always the way it was. So that's all I knew.

Danny Wood was on my bus that first year, but I didn't really know him. I know that Jimbo knew his sister, but we didn't really start hanging out that much in elementary school. We didn't have that many classes together. Till high school really, we were in hardly any of the same classes at all. Middle school's when we started getting together, when we hooked up with these two girls, and that's when we started hanging out.

I was real smart as a kid. I always got good grades, until certain points in my life, when I started goofing around.

Middle school was my favorite, that and my first two years in high school. It was the wildest, the funnest, the craziest. Middle school I was happiest. In high school, I started worrying about things, not important things. When I was in elementary school and middle school, I was worried about doing good work and other things. But when I got into high school, I started worrying about what I looked like. I mean, I always liked to look good, I liked to dress good. In middle school I didn't really care what I looked like. Once, I had some teeth knocked out playing hockey—they were broken in half—but I didn't care, I loved it. Now, they're capped.

In high school I started getting zits and I started caring that I had zits. But one thing I liked about high school was when I got into drama class. We put on some great plays. In one of them, I was the only guy in the whole play—all the rest were girls, but I didn't care. We did one where I played the husband in an interracial marriage and there was a scene where I was apologizing to my wife for the hard life we'd had. It was really moving and I cried real tears.

Sports was my main thing after school when I was in the early grades, anyway. Mostly I played in the streets. I got into organized sports twice. I played basketball once and we lost the championship. And I played baseball one season and we won the championship. That was great. I loved it when we won.

MUSICAL ROOTS

I remember when I first started hearing rap music, I was like, in the fourth grade. And if I wasn't in the school I was, I probably wouldn't have been exposed to it. But I *was* in that school, and that's what the kids were listening to, and that's what I grew up on. And I loved it. My

TOP:
In first grade (courtesy Alma Conroy)

MIDDLE:
In second grade (courtesy Alma Conroy)

BOTTOM:
My first communion at St. Gregory's, 7 years old (courtesy Alma Conroy)

OPPOSITE:
Me with brother Jimbo, 1989 (courtesy Alma Conroy)

musical roots are in rap music and heavy metal music, because my brothers Artie and Paul listened to heavy metal. Artie loved Led Zeppelin, Paul loved AC/DC. Artie really influenced me musically, 'cause he hipped me to the radio and all the music that I started to love, which even then they were playing a lot on the radio. It was good music.

But the kids in school were listening to rap and so was I. People sometimes say, "Oh, what does this white kid know about rap?" Well, what do *they* know about what I know about rap? That's what was in my face every day, hiphop music and I loved hiphop music, y'know? I groove off hiphop music, I appreciate hiphop music. That started way back in elementary school.

And the first time I heard a rap, I wrote a rap. The first one I wrote wasn't really about anything, it was just rap. Me and my brother did it, me and my little brother Mark wrote a rap. We just really stole the idea of "Rapper's Delight," which was the first big commercial rap song. We stole the names and changed them a little, it was funny.

I remember this one called "The Ronald Reagan Rap"—that was the first real song I wrote. It was like five pages long, and I used to know it by heart. I still know a lot of it.

I always liked doing rap, writing rap or just writing rhymes, writing poetry, expressing myself through words, doing it lyrically. Whether I used it in a rock song, a folk song, or a rap song, it's just expressin' myself through music.

I didn't buy too many records. The first record I bought, it was like crazy, it was Maurice Starr's brother's album, *Space Cowboy* by the Jonzon Crew. And it was before I met him. But it was crazy because I went up to the record store and I looked at these albums, and I was stuck between the New Edition and the Jonzon Crew. I was discovering a connection, though, 'cause reading the album covers I kept seeing the name, Maurice Starr, on both albums. And then I saw Maurice Starr's album.

I was in a band when I was about eleven or something. That was called Risk and it was just me and my friends, banging on the drums, and guitars and harmonicas in the garage. Me, Billy, Eric, and Jamie. But sometimes we did something and recorded it on cassette and it would come out good, it would come out kinda interesting.

But we weren't doing it because we thought we'd be famous. It was just fun. I was always doin' things like that, though. If I found a tape recorder, I would talk on it a lot. I always had a good imagination. When I played army, I played army—I didn't play around. I got really into it. I mean I wouldn't have all the equipment and stuff, but I believed what I was doing.

> **" All I thought about when I was a teenager was girls. I always had a girl, I could always get a girl ...They've always been important to me...I've had my heart broken, but in those days I was a heartbreaker too. "**

> **Everyone has this impression of me as this wild kid, but actually I was a lot more quiet when I was little... it took a lot for me to go up and talk to people.**

I got into Michael Jackson in the ninth grade. At first, I wasn't as into Michael Jackson as I had people believin', but it brought so much attention to me—the girls, the girls would always come up to me. His *Thriller* album was real popular at the time. I had sixty-five buttons and at least four hundred posters of him; pictures all over all four walls of my bedroom. See the fans today, they think they got their walls covered, but they couldn't hang with what I had of Michael Jackson. I had a "Beat It" jacket, T-shirts, hats. I used to wear loafers, dress just like him, with what I could. See, that was the thing, I didn't have money, so I didn't have the resources, so I took my father's loafers. I imitated the moves, I did the moonwalk, but I didn't sing.

TEEN YEARS

When I was about 13, my parents got divorced. Since I was the kid who always wanted things to go smoothly, I would have preferred if they didn't get divorced. But they did—and you know what? A lot of really good things came out of it. I was lucky because my dad didn't move too far away. He was right in the neighborhood and I could see him every day if I wanted to, but just on weekends and things like that. We'd have, like, two Christmases; one at mom's and one at dad's. In some ways, me and my dad had an even better relationship after the divorce.

And when my mom re-married, she married a really great guy. My step-dad, Mark Conroy, never tried to take over my father's role, he never overruled what my dad said or anything like that. Instead, he's always been a friend to me and my brothers and sisters. Like I said, we've been real lucky with the whole thing.

In the seventh grade, I met The Kool Aid Bunch, just a posse of kids and that was a real turning point for me. There was Danny Wood, Elliot, Joe [not McIntyre], David, and Chris Knight, Jordan's brother. I wasn't in school with Jordan and Jon at this time, and I didn't hang with Chris because he was their brother, I just hung with him because he was Chris Knight and I liked him.

I always hated people who tried to do things just to look cool. And I did it too. I smoked just to be a cool guy and I understand why I did that. I never got into the habit of smoking, it was just something I did to try and be cool. And when I was real young, being cool was important, but when I met the Kool Aid Bunch, I wasn't worried about bein' cool anymore. Just being with those guys made me real loose. When I started to hang with them, I found out that being tough wasn't all that important. Just being *me* was important. And the things I didn't want

people to know about, suddenly it didn't matter if they did know about them.

Like now I'll say, "Yeah, *Sesame Street*'s my favorite TV show." Most people my age, guys, wouldn't say that, but I don't care. It's not really my favorite TV show, but I just say it. It kind of is, when I think about it, it's one of them.

Danny Wood and me were cool. I would hang with him after school and stuff like that, drive on the bus with him and go on dates with him and two girls. We would double-date.

All I thought about when I was a teenager was girls. I always had a girl, I could always get a girl. I did pretty good when I was younger, I did good with the girls. They've always been important to me. I liked taking the subway to new neighborhoods to meet new girls. I was shy, but I'd make a lot of eye contact first, then slowly start telling jokes and getting all the attention. I was a big flirt, and pretty soon the girl would be interested in me. I've had my heart broken, but in those days, I was a heartbreaker too.

A lot of people have described me as a street kid, but I'm not trying to be known as a street kid—I'm just trying to be known as *me*. I just grew up hanging out in the streets. That's what I know. I know people say, "Oh, Maurice Starr wanted some street smart kids for the group." It doesn't matter whether he wanted street smart kids or not 'cause that's just what I am. If I wasn't in the group, I'd still be that. So it's not like Maurice Starr trained us to be street smart kids, that's what I am.

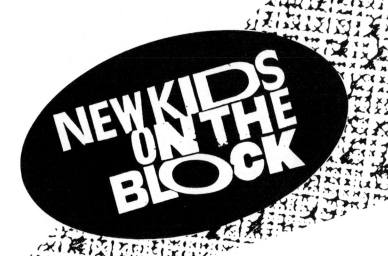

JORDAN KNIGHT

I was born in Worcester, Massachusetts, on May 17, 1970. We didn't live there, that's just where the hospital was. My mom, Marlene, comes from Canada, and she always wanted to give one of her children names that represented the two cultures of Canada, English and French. So my full name is Jordan Nathaniel Marcel Knight. I was the sixth child in the family. Before me were Allison, Sharon, David, Christopher, and Jonathan.

The first house I lived in was in a Boston suburb called Westwood. In that house all four of us boys shared one bunk bed, two on top and two on the bottom. I always shared with Jonathan.

I was close to all my brothers and sisters, but growing up, I was closer to different ones at different times. I was always close to Jonathan. I was close to Dave when I was very little and then again when I was around ten years old. Dave and I used to play soccer together, we used to be in the neighborhood leagues. I

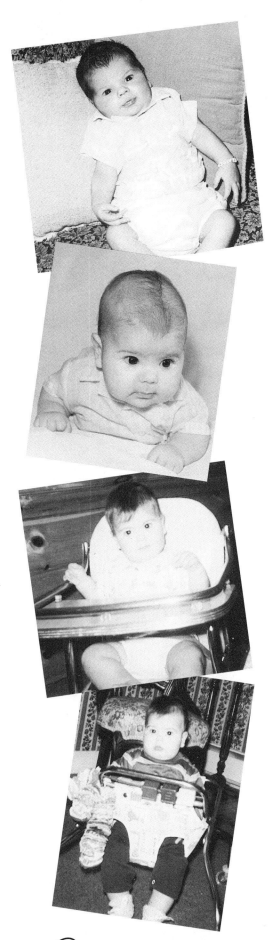

think sports brought us together and music too. We liked the same music.

Then, around twelve, thirteen, I started bein' real close to Chris. We would hang out with the same people, and we went out a lot together.

Even though I was closest to my brothers, I'm really most like my sister Allison in my personality. Allison is real quiet, real shy, and I think we both have the same problem with communicating with people one-on-one. I have a lot of trouble talkin' to individuals and havin' a conversation with one person. But yet when I get on stage, in front of 15,000 people, I just let loose. It's really weird and I don't understand it.

I was *tiny* back then. I used to be the littlest kid. I used to look like a girl, with this long curly hair, and when I would walk into stores, people wouldn't know what to call me, a boy or a girl. I had chubby cheeks and stuff, and everyone used to love grabbing my cheeks.

My dad, Allan, was a carpenter and also a minister. When we lived in Westwood, he had his own church where he was the preacher. My mom is a social worker who specialized in family therapy.

I was lucky to have the parents I did, 'cause they weren't strict, not at all. They always really *cared*, we always knew that they cared, but they let us do what we wanted to do and be independent. As long as we got our chores done and stuff, that is. When I'm a parent someday, I think I'll be like them.

When I was almost three, we moved to this really big old house in Dorchester. It had something like seventeen rooms and ten bedrooms. People used to get lost when they'd come to my house! But in the beginning, there were other people living in the house, it was three families. So at first, it was crowded, real squishy, and all the boys were still in the same room. This time we had two beds, not bunk beds. But I was still sharing with Jonathan. Eventually, the other two families moved out and we had the whole house. But I didn't get to have my own room then—in fact, I didn't have my own room until I was sixteen—'cause when the other families moved out, I started sharing with foster kids that came to live with us.

AN EXTENDED FAMILY

It seems like as long as I could remember there were foster kids in the house. When I was little, I didn't think about it. They were people, they just lived with us, it was part of life. Later on, I found out that my mom was doing this for professional *and* for personal reasons. As a social worker, she created this program, a family-oriented group residence for disturbed teenagers, kids that for one reason or another had kind of "flunked out" of traditional foster-care homes. She ran this program

out of our house. But she wasn't only doing this because it was her career. She was doing it out of her heart. She believes deeply that "there has to be a place for every kid," and the place she created happened to be at our house.

There were some times when there were fourteen, fifteen people in the house. Our house was so wild that people could come over anytime and be entertained, because so much was going on. Sometimes it bugged me. I could never get a free moment or time to myself, 'cause there was always something going on.

We didn't only have kids, either. We had elderly and disabled people too. A couple of elderlys died while they were living with us.

We have a guy, Ken, who still lives with us who was in a car crash. He was an alcoholic and lost his memory of everything after the car crash. But he's real, real smart, and before the accident he was studying to become a doctor. I used to bring my homework to him and he'd do it with me—but he couldn't remember what he did five minutes ago.

Some of the foster kids were addicted, some were abused, some had serious mental problems. There were all types. Some lived with us for years, and I've gotten very close to a lot of them. When I was little, the foster girls would cook for me, just like in a real family. A lot of them were happy to be in our house because they had never seen anything like it before. Some foster parents are real strict and do it only for the money and don't have the loving frame of mind my mother has. She was doing this out of her heart, but she kept control. Believe me, she's a strong woman and didn't take junk from any of them. If they swore, they got punished same as we did. She kept everyone in line. She would try to keep on top of everyone about doing their homework, but it was kinda hard.

A lot of them still keep in touch and even come to my mother for advice. So that shows that she really did good for them. And I think that the ones I got close to are real, real proud of us now.

I never felt bad towards the foster kids. I was never jealous of any of them, and I never resented them being there. But there was a lot of stress. The only times we had big problems was if any of them did something real bad, like steal from us. And that happened. Certain people would do it a lot.

Of course, I felt crowded—big-time. But I was always proud of it all. I used to love when other people would come in and see how crazy my house was. There was never a dull moment!

I think that living with foster kids has given me the personality I have today. I'm very liberal and very open-minded, and I'm not prejudiced one bit—and I think that's what did it. I learned how to get along with anybody.

With so many of us in the house, we all had stuff to do. We had lists of chores, who would cook—different people would cook every night—and who would do the dishes. Up until the time I was ten or eleven, we'd all sit down and have dinners together, saying grace and everything. I usually washed dishes and raked leaves and stuff and cleaned my room. But I never wanted to do any of it. It was more like I just wanted to hang out, go out with my friends. Jon did everything, though. Jonathan just would do stuff because he wanted it done. That's the way he still is today.

SCHOOL DAYS

I started going to school in kindergarten. My whole family, all my sisters and brothers went to the Trotter School, and I did too. A lot has been written saying that we white kids were bused to school in a black neighborhood, but for me it wasn't really like that. See, I don't live in a white neighborhood, I live in a mixed neighborhood, so being bused to Roxbury, where the school was, was nothin' to me. It was only ten minutes by bus, but I could get there on my bike in five minutes. It wasn't the closest school to my house, but if I did go to the closest school, it would've been mixed just the same.

For some other kids who went to Trotter and who came from white neighborhoods, it was a big influential thing for them, but it really didn't have a big influence on me, y'know, I don't see that. For me, growin' up in the house I did, and in the neighborhood I did, it was like normal life. My brother Chris is black and so were a lot of the foster kids in our house. My part of Dorchester is totally mixed. So being bused to Trotter was just normal for me, a kid going to school.

I was on the same bus as Donnie, so I've known him since I was tiny. But I was closer to his younger brother Mark. Mark and I were good

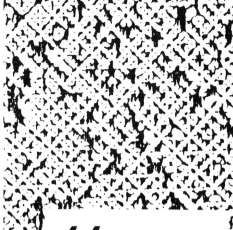

" I'm really most like my sister Allison in personality. Allison is real quiet, real shy, and I think we both have the same problem communicating with people one-on-one...But when I get on stage, in front of 15,000 people, I just let loose. "

friends, we used to hang out. When we were little, though, I used to think of Donnie as a bully. He never bothered with me, except he'd come over and pinch my cheeks and say, "Jordan! You're so *cute!*"

I was pretty good in school. I liked math, and I used to read a lot. I still like reading. I think I'm smart. I think that I probably absorbed more than the kids who got all A's and stuff even if my grades weren't always that great. I've always been fascinated with everything, fascinated with learning, but I didn't always want to do the work, didn't always want to do my homework or a report. But when the teacher talked, I listened. I was fascinated.

What I liked best about the Trotter School is that we had a lot of art and we always had plays. My first play was *Charlie and the Chocolate Factory.* I was in the fourth grade and I was Charlie, the leading role. I used to love seeing the plays that the other classes put on. There'd be a night show and a day show, all the parents came, and it was great. I loved it.

Trotter had a great chorus, and you had to try out to be in it. They'd put on musicals and stuff, and that used to be fun. I used to love doing that. I made the chorus right away and it's funny—the lady always used to try and make me do solos, but I was so shy. One day the soloist she usually used was absent and she made me sing. The kids couldn't believe how high I sang. I was so embarrassed, because they were blown away by how high I was singing. Everyone stared at me and I was so embarrassed I never did it again.

FRIENDS & GAMES

I didn't make friends easily, but I was a likable person. People didn't have trouble getting along with me at all, and I get along with people real easily, even if they're real different. Some people don't want to be friends with people if they're different than they are, but it never mattered to me. I've always been nice to everyone in school. It would take me a long time to make friends because I was reserved. But once I got to know someone, it was okay.

Looking back on it, I think I was popular. I must've cared about being popular, 'cause I always wanted to look good.

After school I was always pretty busy. When I was a real little boy I used to go to choir practice for church three days a week. And I used to play Little League baseball and hockey. I was into a lot of different things when I was little—soccer, basketball, all sports, in school and in town. When I was little, I was into all the extracurricular stuff, but as I grew older, I strayed away from that.

In my neighborhood, we played street games. Our favorite was Kick

The Can. This is how you play. One person finds a soda can in the street and guides it with his foot while the others hide. You gotta make boundaries, and the guy guiding the can would have to spot you and say your name while he was touching the can. But while he was looking for you, you could run to the can and kick it away from him. Then you were free, and everyone he caught before goes free. That's a common game for city kids.

When I got older and got into breakdancing, we'd go to this warehouse and get big cardboard boxes that they used to store refrigerators and stuff, and we'd dance on the cardboard. You could set your box up right in the street or in a playground and dance on it.

HARD TIMES

There were a lot of fun times and good memories, but it definitely wasn't easy for us. We never had much money and sometimes, we didn't have heat during the winter. We slept with electric blankets to keep us warm. I don't want to make it sound like we were totally poor, 'cause there are so many people who are much poorer. And I don't want to sound like I'm feeling sorry for myself, because we weren't that bad off. There are people a hundred times worse off than we were.

But there were times when there was no heat and a lack of food—there were so many mouths to feed, that's what it was. Like, a lot of times I'd go to my friend's house and eat. He reminded me of that re-

TOP:
Ten years old (courtesy Marlene Putman)

MIDDLE:
Me and Allison, May 1979 (courtesy Marlene Putman)

LEFT:
Sister Allison washing the car and us (courtesy Marlene Putman)

> I never really thought about becoming famous, even though I loved singing. I always sang around the house when I was a kid. Everybody told me I had a good voice.

cently. He also told me that no one in the neighborhood would ever want to sleep over my house because there was no heat. I think I knew that, but I didn't let it bother me.

I don't know if I felt bad about not having a lot, but when New Edition, the singing group, came out of Boston, I used to always look at the clothes they had and the sneakers they wore and be real envious. They had gold chains, and I'd look at their gold chains and say, "Man, I wish I could buy a gold chain." But now that I've got some money and stuff, it's really nothin' to me. Now that I look back, I can see that's not what it's all about, really.

FAMILY TRIPS

We might not have had money, but we were together, for the most part. Every Christmas we used to go to Canada to visit my family. Then every summer we went to my Grandma and Grandpa Putman's cottage on Lake Erie in Ontario. Ever since my mother was little, she went to that cottage in the summers, so it was sort of like a family tradition.

We all piled in a station wagon—it was crowded—and drove up. It was about an eight- or ten-hour drive. It's long, but it's nothin' compared to the drives we do now when we're on tour!

Both sets of my grandparents lived in Ontario, so we'd see all the family. We also visited my cousin's farm when we were there and that was real fun—we had the best times. We'd ride horses, and they had everything: chickens, pigs, cows, all types of animals. We jumped from the haylofts and stuff like that, sold corn that we picked down at the road, drove through the corn patch on a motorcycle, crazy stuff. It was so different from what we were used to in the city, so fascinating, so fun!

MUSICAL INFLUENCES

When I was young I went to church every week. The whole family went. It was like the church was the center of the family, which was a good thing. Dad started out as a Baptist preacher and then, when we moved to Dorchester and joined the Episcopal church, he was ordained at our church, All Saints Episcopal in the Ashmont section of Dorchester. All of us and our Mom go there, but our Dad is in a parish outside of Boston.

For me, especially when I was little, the best thing about church was the choir. It was called the All Saints Episcopal Church Choir, and it was part of the Royal School of Church Music. It had very high standards. You had to try out to be in it, but I didn't really have to try out.

That's because the choirmaster, Herb Peterson, was a friend of the family's and he knew I could sing. I couldn't wait to be old enough to join the choir, and when I was six, I did. I loved it, it was fun, and we used to do all kinds of things, like take trips. There were about thirty-five kids in the choir. The soprano section was all boys, and I was in that one. That's where I got my falsetto voice from.

Herb Peterson was a really big influence on me. I wouldn't say he taught me to sing, because I don't think anyone can teach anybody how to sing. You gotta have it in you to sing, and I always did.

But Herb, and my mother, too, really instilled in me the importance of being a perfectionist. Herb taught me to "make it perfect." We practiced three times a week and sang at mass. And it was one of the best choirs around. On Christmas, we'd have an organ, trumpets, French horns, timpani drums, and we traveled to other churches to perform. I remember I had some favorite liturgies and I'd go to the choirmaster and ask to do them. Mostly, I loved a lot of Mozart's mass music.

I was a soloist at church. Jonathan and I were head co-choristers. A chorister is a young boy who sings the treble section. Usually there was only one head chorister and he was the soloist, but not in this case.

But I remember I would get scared, boy, getting ready to sing a solo. One time I didn't show up—I was so scared, it was crazy! I just went to the bathroom and never came out! I got over my fear; I don't get scared now going onstage. But I gotta feel comfortable with the situation first.

One summer, Jonathan and I went to the Royal School of Church Music Camp in Princeton, New Jersey. It was an honor to be chosen to go there, because only the most promising choristers were picked. And we got some heavy-duty training that summer; we also sang at all the masses in the cathedral.

TOP LEFT:
At the amusement park with brothers Jonathan, David, and Chris (courtesy Marlene Putman)

TOP RIGHT:
(courtesy Marlene Putman)

ABOVE:
In our choir robes (courtesy Marlene Putman)

The family at Thanksgiving 1989—Back row: brother Christopher, his fiancée Kerry, nephew Matthew (Sharon's son), Jonathan, sister Allison, our friend Richard. Front row: Grandpa Putman, Grandma Putman, Mom, Jordan, brother David, sister Sharon. (© 1989 Larry Busacca)

I never really thought about becoming famous, even though I loved singing. I always sang around the house when I was a kid. Everyone always told me I had a good voice. I'd be singing all the time. I'd be in the subway station, and everyone knew me as the little kid who sang music all the time. I used to sing Beatles songs and such when I was little.

I've always had an appreciation for good music. When I was six and seven years old, I loved the Beatles' music; they were oldies by then. My older sisters and brothers had records, and I listened to what they listened to. Me and my brother Dave—he sang too—had the same appreciation for music. That's what really made us close when I was little. He would get a new album and we'd sit down and listen to it together.

I never went to a concert. I just liked the music, I was never into the artist or anything, really. But I remember one time, the one concert I did want to go to, my whole family went and I couldn't go. It was Elton John (I remember this vividly), I was like five or six, and I wanted to go so badly, but they said I was too little.

My graduation from English High School, June 14, 1988 (courtesy Marlene Putman)

RAP & BREAKDANCING

The first record I bought was probably a rap record. When rap first started out, I was into it right away. "Rapper's Delight" was the first big commercial rap song, and our whole bus going to school used to chant it. It was like the real early stages of rap and I was into it, big-time. In the early days, I liked Grandmaster Flash & The Furious Five and Malcolm McLaren.

I was into breakdancing even before it became real commercial. When it did become commercial a little later on, I'd watch these kids on TV breakdancing and I used to wonder how they got on TV, because we were so much better. We were into the core, street stuff.

No one would teach you breakdancing, because if you copied somebody's move, you were, like, no good. You don't copy, you've got to be original. So no one would teach their moves because they'd think you'd steal from them. So what you'd have to do is sit there and pretend you're not looking at the kid dancing—just look out of the corner of your eye and then go practice in your room at home.

TEEN YEARS

I went through a wild period as a teenager. I hung out on the streets. I really think that I, more than any of the kids in the group, was most into the street. You might not see that by lookin' at the group now, but that's true. I didn't do anything real, real bad, but I'd go to parties, come in real late, not come home at all. I was really into mostly just hangin' out. I'd ride the trains all night, write my name all over the train. We were on the trains so much, we practically knew how to drive them. It's just kind of a thing that city kids do. Me and my friends, we'd all get together and do different schemes. Jonathan was never a part of it, he wasn't a part of my group. He was into different things.

When I was a teenager, my parents got divorced. I don't really like to talk about that, and it bothers me when people make assumptions. It's just nobody's business, really. That's how I feel about it.

After elementary school, I went to the Thayer Academy for junior high school, which is in Braintree, Massachusetts, a suburb of Boston. Then I started at Catholic Memorial for high school, but I didn't like it, it wasn't my type of school. First, it was all boys, which I didn't like, and second, they told you what you had to wear. It wasn't a uniform, but you had to wear shoes (no sneakers), and a shirt with a collar and all.

But the bigger problem was that a lot of the kids there—not all of them—would make fun of me for the clothes I wore and because I hung around with black kids and Puerto Rican kids and they didn't want to accept that. Not all of them, but most would make fun of me. I get along with most people, but if people don't get along with me, I don't even want to be around them. And that's how it was really. I felt totally isolated at that time, I was really lonely. I didn't do a lot of school work, I didn't want to be there. So eventually I left that school and went to English High, which was fine.

The things that mattered most to me in those days were girls, parties, and breakdancing, I was going through a period where I didn't care about anything else. But that was about to change, big-time!

" Nobody would teach you break-dancing, because if you copied someone's move, you were no good. You don't copy, you've got to be original... So what you'd have to do is sit there and pretend you're not looking at the kid dancing— just look out of the corner of your eye and then go practice in your room at home. "

(© 1990 Larry Busacca)

KIDSTUFF: CHAPTER THREE

JOSEPH McINTYRE

I was supposed to be named Christopher. That's the name my mom had picked out when she was pregnant with me. But on the day I was born—December 31, 1972, at Glover Hospital in Needham, Massachusetts—my dad marched into the hospital and said to my mom, "His name is Joseph Mulrey." That was the name of a close family friend, and my dad suddenly decided he wanted to name me after him. I've got seven older sisters and one older brother, Tommy, who's named after my dad. The house I grew up in is the same one my family has always lived in. It's in Jamaica Plain, which is a neighborhood in Boston. It's not too far from Dorchester, but it's very different.

My parents are Katherine—everybody calls her Kay—and Thomas. My dad's a bricklayer. He's President of the Bricklayers' Union for the New England area and Vice President of the national Bricklayers' Union. And while I was growing up, my

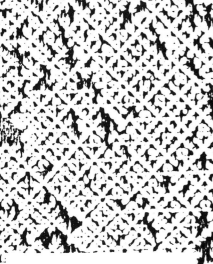

> **"Since I was the youngest, my sisters always kept a special eye on me. My brother played with me a lot. I think he was glad to have a brother, after all those sisters."**

mom was a house mother, she just did everything for us. My mother always calls me Joseph. She says Joe McIntyre sounds like a fighter or something. Most of my friends, all my life, have just called me Joe or Joey. Okay, my sisters—in descending order they are: Judith, Alice, Susan, Patricia, Carol, Jean, and Kate. My brother Tommy is four years older than I am.

Our house was crowded and we all had to share bedrooms. By the time I was born, Judith was eighteen and she'd already left. She moved to New York to become an actress, and she's real talented. She's been on afternoon TV in *The Guiding Light* and *One Life to Live*. So after she left, my parents converted the attic into bedrooms for my sisters. My brother and I shared "the little room," as my mother called it. We had bunk beds. My brother kind of took control of the decorating, you might say. Mostly we had sports posters all over the walls. We were big Boston College fans, especially since my father had season tickets to their football games.

We were fans of all the Boston pro teams, too—the Patriots, and the Red Sox for baseball. I remember going to my first Red Sox game when I was very little—I fell asleep right in the stands! Even though it was a big household, we were close. Everyone came together for dinner at 5:30 every day. We always sat the same way around the dining room table. Me and my mom would be at one end, my dad and my brother on the other, and the girls in the middle. We had beans and franks every Saturday. My mother cooked for everyone, and like all mothers who have to feed so many kids, she never ate, she never sat down with the family. I don't know how she did it.

My sisters usually helped clean up and stuff, washed the dishes, swept the steps, and all. But I was the baby and I never really had a chore—neither did my brother. I don't even remember having to clean my room, 'cause my mom pretty much did everything. But the girls never complained about it, you know, about the boys not doing anything. My mom is from the old school, where guys don't help with the housework. She jokes that by the time I came along, there was nothing left to do anyway!

Since I was the youngest, my sisters always kept a special eye on me. My brother played with me a lot. I think he was glad to have a brother, after all those sisters. Sometimes he wouldn't take me along when he was going with his friends—that always happens with younger brothers, I guess—but we used to do all sorts of games together. We'd play football in the parlor and Nerf Ball in my parents' bedroom. We'd kind of sneak around doing that, 'cause we really weren't allowed to. He was a good older brother, especially for a little kid.

MY BIGGEST TREASURE

It wasn't hard for me to get attention. I don't know, I guess I had a good sense of humor and I made people laugh, stuff like that. I never felt crowded, either. I love big families. Family is everything to me, that's my biggest treasure, my family. That's why I love Christmas so much, 'cause everyone comes together. Just like when we were little, everyone came to my house for Christmas. They still do now, only now it's more special, 'cause my three oldest sisters don't live in Boston anymore. Judith is in New York, Alice is in Vermont, and Susan's in Miami. But we all come together.

I used to love that feeling, when I'd be the first one up on Christmas Day and just wake everyone up. Everyone would come down, be squishy and stuff. And I was the little one, so I could go wherever I wanted.

When I have a family someday, *if* I have a family, I'd like it to be relatively big.

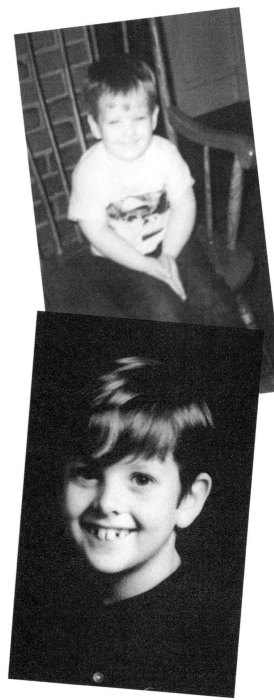

TOP:
Three years old, January 1976, in my Elton John t-shirt (courtesy Kay McIntyre)

BOTTOM:
School picture time—2nd grade (courtesy Kay McIntyre)

OPPOSITE:
With my mom at 1989 concert at Great Woods (courtesy Kay McIntyre)

MY BEST BIRTHDAY EVER & MY FIRST TRAUMA

Birthdays were a pretty big deal in our house, you could say. Everyone brought presents for the birthday child. I'll never forget my favorite birthday. I was six years old, and I can see it right here. I wasn't sitting in my usual spot. For some reason I was sitting where the girls sit. The door to the kitchen was right there. And I was sitting facing it. And what I really wanted for my birthday was a Charlie McCarthy doll, a puppet that the famous ventriloquist Edgar Bergen used. I think I remember hearing stories that my father used to have one when he was a kid. I'm not sure if that's why I wanted it, I just did.

Suddenly, from out of the kitchen, my mother and father brought in a brand-new Charlie McCarthy doll. I was so overjoyed. I mean, it was unbelievable. My face lit up like a Christmas tree. And I will never forget when they gave it to me. My family was all around, my parents right there with the doll. It was the greatest feeling.

I loved that doll. Then, I think I was around eight years old, and my brother and sister were play-fighting, Tommy and my sister Jean. I think this was my first traumatic experience. They were fighting and they rolled on the doll. And I was going to get it from under them, so I grabbed the arm and pulled on it—and I ended up with just the arm. I had ripped it right off. And I was just so upset, I was sobbing, I was screaming. I don't think I'd ever been that upset about anything.

Later on I pinned the arm back on, but it was never the same. It was just all floppy.

TOP LEFT:
At sister Judith's party, with sister Patricia (courtesy Kay McIntyre)

TOP RIGHT:
Surrounded by six of my seven sisters! (courtesy Kay McIntyre)

BOTTOM LEFT:
Singing at my sister Carol's wedding 1988 (courtesy Kay McIntyre)

OPPOSITE:
Early days as a New Kid (© 1986 CBS Records, Inc. Courtesy Columbia Records)

THINGS WE DID TOGETHER

As you might expect with so many kids, there were squabbles and different rivalries all the time. I was close to different sisters for different reasons. Carol and I have a lot of the same interests. My sister Alice is my godmother. She gave me most of my spiritual guidance in my younger years. She taught me a lot about God and stuff like that. So that was real special. I had a nice relationship with her. When she was going to college, Alice and I used to have breakfast together every morning. She was wild about Elton John—she dressed up like him for Halloween one year—and she'd teach me Elton John songs over breakfast. We'd sing them together.

My sister Susan and I used to go for walks together. Tricia, well, we're friends now, but back then, I never really hung around with her a lot. She was just a teenager and she didn't really pay a lot of attention to me. And I never really lived with Judy, so I didn't really know her. I remember one thing though: she always said I looked like a chicken when I was born.

Jean and I would cuddle up under the covers with our favorite snack of cocoa, peanut butter, and crackers, and we'd sing songs together. And Kate was the sister closest to my age. She and Tommy and I would play board games together.

Every summer we'd go to Cape Cod for vacation, and then other times of the year, we'd go to a lot of conventions for my dad's job. He'd get a big business car, like a big Chevrolet or something, and we would just pack it up and go. My dad and I used to sing in the car—I'd stand behind him and we'd sing "New York, New York" together. That was a lot of fun for me. My sisters didn't think so. They'd be saying, "Oh, my God, get me out of here," because they were teenagers and wanted to be with their friends. I was loving every minute of it. We got to stay in hotels and I thought that was fun.

I was definitely my mother's boy when I was young. She took me under her wing. I was with her all the time. It's going to take a long time for her to let go!

But my brother and my father and I did a lot together. We went to games and played football in the street. My dad worked long hours, though. That was probably my mom's biggest complaint. When I was young, I wanted to be a bricklayer like my dad; that's what my brother does now. He's an apprentice. If I hadn't gotten into the group, I would have taken it up as a skill, but I definitely would have gone to college first. My brother wasn't that keen on school. He's a bright kid and everything, but he wasn't that interested.

My parents weren't really strict with us kids. There was an under-

> " Performing was just something I did, pretty steadily, with rehearsals every Friday night. It was just fun, a part of my life. The one thing I loved more than anything else was the applause. "

standing about what was right and what was wrong. They were kind of cool. I mean, every once in a while they would say no, but not too often. If I asked for something, my father usually said, "Ask your mother," and my mother would usually let me do whatever it was I wanted.

The only thing she would never let me do is get a pet. I wanted a kitten, and I was allergic to cats. But when my friend's cat had kittens, I wanted one. I kept badgering my mom, and I really thought she was going to give in, but she never did. When I was real little we had a poodle, but it only lasted a week in our house—we gave it away 'cause the kids were supposed to take care of it, but we didn't.

GOING TO CHURCH

My mother's a very devout Catholic, and church has always been real important to her. My dad too. We belonged to St. Thomas Aquinas Church and we'd all go, every Sunday. Sometimes I went twice, once with my mother in the morning, and then to late mass with my father and brother.

When I was about six or seven, I joined the church choir, which I really liked. When I was ten I became an altar boy. A lot of kids did that. We helped the priest—we held the Bible for him to read, brought up the bread and wine, stuff like that.

I still go to church with my family whenever I'm home, whenever I can.

TOP LEFT:
My confirmation in September 1989—my brother Tom was my sponsor (courtesy Kay McIntyre)

TOP RIGHT:
At my sister Patricia's wedding in 1988 (courtesy Kay McIntyre)

OPPOSITE:
I love Christmas! (© 1989 Larry Busacca)

GOING TO SCHOOL

I started school in kindergarten. I went to the Agassiz School, which was just near my house. What I remember most about kindergarten is that it was a half-day and my mother used to pick me up every day and take me out to lunch. We had three favorite places that we liked to go.

From grades one through eight, I went to St. Mary's of Assumption School in Brookline, which is a suburb of Boston. A lot of kids from Jamaica Plain went there. We took a bus, but it wasn't like being bused the way the others in the group were. This was a charter and St. Mary's was a parochial school, not a public school.

I always got good grades. That was never a problem for me—A's and B's all the way through. St. Mary's was kind of a breeze, really. So my mother never got on me for my grades. It was my conduct she was worried about. I was a little bit of a discipline problem. I didn't do anything really bad. I wasn't the class clown or anything. I mean, I'd make a few jokes every once in a while and I always had a good sense of humor. Me and my friends in school were part of what you might call the "hip crowd." We were always making people laugh. But the main thing was that I had no self-control. I'd always be getting out of my seat and talking out of turn.

PLAY TIME

I didn't really have a huge number of friends. It was just me and my best friend, you know. He lived across the street. And we hung around, we were just alike. It was like a perfect relationship, you know how it is with best friends. I wasn't shy at all—coming from such a big family, I had kind of a big personality.

We used to play in Kelly's Circle, which was a little circle up the street by my house. There's a big highway around it. And then there was a place called Jamaica Pond that had a bike path and a running track where we played. We'd play games like Kick The Can and all kinds of sports. One of my favorite things to do in the winter was go ice skating with my friends. There was a rink in the next town that we used to walk to.

The only time I ever joined organized sports was in the second grade. My brother was in football all his life and I tried Pop Warner football, which is the youngest division. I had the coordination and stuff, but I only stayed on the team for a month. Then I quit. I just didn't want to do it. I think you have to be brought up for that stuff. And I wasn't really a big kid. So I just played with my brother and with my friends. Those were the kinds of sports I loved.

T O P :
(© 1989 Larry Busacca)

B O T T O M :
With my sister Carol, who shares my New Year's Eve birthday—here she's 20 and I'm 10
(courtesy Kay McIntyre)

A SHOW-BIZ KID

My mother was always into acting and singing. She did some when she was in high school, but didn't try for a career in it. She dropped it to be a mother. She picked it up again right before I was born. It just so happened that we lived on the same street as the Footlight Club, which is the oldest community theater in America. My mom had never even realized that it was there, but some people in her church group were involved, and when they asked if anyone else was interested in acting, she jumped at the chance to get back on the stage. She actually did her very first play there when she was pregnant with me, so I always feel that I was kinda destined for this business in a way. She really loved it, and she's been doing plays there all these years. It didn't take long before more of my family got involved. At first my sisters would come and serve the cocoa and clean up, do the dirty work. But soon they started performing too.

My sister Carol really got into it, and she was the one who encouraged me. See, we were born on the same day, ten years apart, so there's kind of a bond between us.

When I was six, the director of our church choir started something called The Neighborhood Children's Theater of Boston—the NCT—and that was my first time on stage. Carol and I did this song together, from the play *Oliver!* That first time there was no acting, just that song in a variety show. That was it. My mom was in the audience that first time and she cried when she heard us singing together. And then I went to the Footlight Club, and that's where I did most of the more serious acting.

But I did *Oliver!* with the NCT, and then again at the Footlight Club. I did *The Music Man*—I played Little Winthrop—and I was also in *Our Town*. And I did a lot of stuff over there and just kept myself busy. I didn't even really think about it—I didn't think about becoming famous, I just went.

No one was really saying to me, "Oh, you have a great voice" or "You should be a singer" or anything. I mean, there was always music in my house, but nobody went around singing big-time. Besides, I think everyone can sing, really. Performing was just something I did, pretty steadily, with rehearsals every Friday night. It was just fun, a part of my life. The one thing I loved more than anything was the applause. I just liked it. But after the show, I'd go home and I really wouldn't talk about it. I never thought about going for singing or acting lessons or anything like that. I guess maybe deep in my heart I wanted to—I still sing from my throat which isn't the way you're supposed to; my sisters know how to sing the right way—but I never did, really.

TOP:
Starring in *Oliver!* at nine years old (courtesy Kay McIntyre)

BOTTOM:
Oliver! again at age eleven (courtesy Kay McIntyre)

It's funny when I think about it. I was doing real well in community theater, getting all kinds of roles, but in school I never made the plays or musicals. I tried out, but I never got any parts.

MIDDLE-SCHOOL BLUES

When I was in sixth grade I took a test for middle school. If you did good, you could qualify for some top schools. I did great on most tests, but I wasn't the quickest reader. I didn't get into the best school, but I got into another pretty tough one called the Latin Academy. I was supposed to go there for middle school and high school. I started, and went from September to March, but I did terrible. It was so hard, it was like going from sixth grade to ninth, that's how advanced it was. And so much homework! I wasn't prepared at all, my grades were terrible and I wasn't into it. It was such a big school.

So I went back to St. Mary's in the middle of seventh grade and stayed until the end of eighth. I did real well there. I got a little scholarship, those funds you get for good grades and stuff.

HANGIN' TOUGH IN HIGH SCHOOL

In ninth grade, I started at Catholic Memorial, which is an all-boys school. But ninth was the only grade I actually spent in the classroom, because I was already in New Kids. By that summer, our record had finally taken off and I had to hit the road. But I remember ninth grade real well, 'cause I was getting straight A's. My report card that whole ninth year was honor roll.

It's weird, 'cause that's when we were recording *Hangin' Tough*. I really had no idea what was going to happen with it. Our first album didn't do so well, and it was iffy whether or not the second one was going to make it. So I was just concentrating on school at that point, 'cause that's what meant the most to me. I did a few shows with New Kids and stuff, but I never really missed school. I mean, every once in a while I'd take a day off to go to New York, but that was it. Basically I was in the classroom in ninth grade, and I did real well. I loved school; anything you do well in, you love.

I never really told the kids at school that I was in a band. I never said a word about it. I mean, we would do a show in the Boston area, often late at night. I'd get home sometimes at four in the morning, sleep for two hours, get up and go to school, and never say a word about it. I might tell my best friend that I did a show the night before, but that was it. I'm not really sure why I didn't tell anyone. It was an all-boys school, and I was thinking back then that they probably wouldn't have

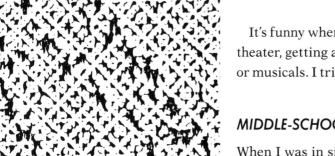

> **I think I'd like to go to college eventually, but wouldn't do it on the road. I'd wait until I could go full-time.**

My family at Thanksgiving 1989—Back row: sister Jean, friend Jimmy, sister Carol, her husband Joe, Dad, me, brother Tom, sister Kate, sister Tricia. Front row: sister Judy, sister Alice, sister Susan, and Mom. (© 1989 Larry Busacca)

cared if I'd told them anyway. They'd never heard of New Kids On The Block.

I never did anything extracurricular in high school, in the one year I was there. I didn't hang around school. I would just go to classes and then come home. I didn't really get into doing stuff.

Anyway, by the spring of my ninth year, things were starting to cook with the band. I remember starting to tell people that we were going to try out to go on tour with Tiffany. The boys in school had heard of Tiffany, so that's when they started getting interested. What happened was, of course, we made the tour, and that's what I did the whole summer. And then I never came back to school for tenth grade.

That was a big conflict for my mother, because up until that time I was able to do school and the band together, and as long as I got good grades, it was okay with her. But in the fall when I was supposed to go to tenth grade, that was when I could no longer do the two things at once. "Please Don't Go Girl" was hitting the Top Ten that September and we needed to continue with the tour. My mother was saying, "Oh, no, you're going to school." My mother was real nervous, 'cause, after all, who knew if New Kids was going to make it? Like most parents, all she worried about was my education.

Finally, we worked it out. We got a tutor, and I've been working with him ever since. And it's cool, I'm doing good. I think I'd like to go to college eventually, but I wouldn't do it on the road. I'd wait until I could go full-time. But the way things are going, I don't know when that's gonna be.

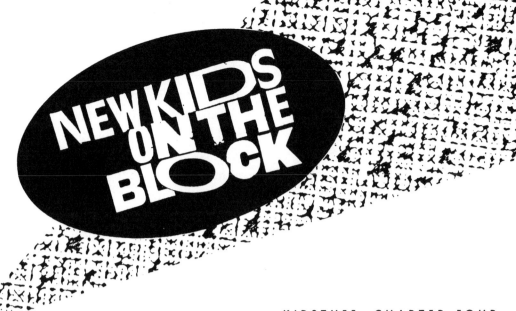

KIDSTUFF: CHAPTER FOUR

JONATHAN
KNIGHT

My full name is Jonathan Rashleigh Knight (my middle name is my grandmother's maiden name), and just like Jordan, I was born in the town of
Worcester, Massachusetts, in the same hospital. It was November 29, 1968. I
lived in a town called Lancaster until I was three years old. Then I moved to
Westwood. In 1973 we moved to Dorchester, where I've been living since
then.

My mom is Marlene, my dad's name is Allan, and my older sisters are
Allison and Sharon. My two older brothers are David and Chris. Then
there's Jordan, who's eighteen months younger than me. My sister
Sharon has a five-year-old son, Matthew, who's a real important
member of the family. And we all live at home with our Mom. My
brother Christopher has two little girls and two little boys. People
usually refer to me as Jon, but I really prefer Jonathan.

Growing up, I was always closest to Jordan. We went to the

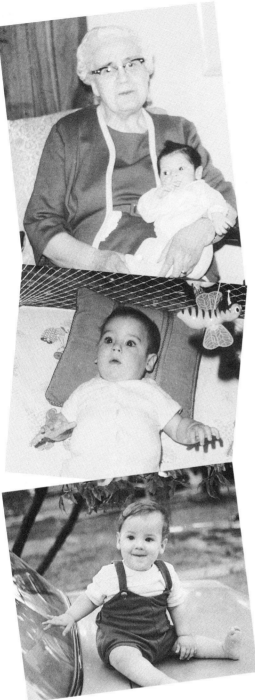

TOP:
Grandma with baby Jonathan, January 1969 (courtesy Marlene Putman)

MIDDLE:
June 1969—Six months old (courtesy Marlene Putman)

BOTTOM:
I like this car—can I drive it? Me at 10 months old (courtesy Marlene Putman)

same schools and when we were little, we used to share a room. I know when we were growing up in Westwood, all four of us, me and Jordan and my two older brothers, shared one room. Jordan and I slept in the bottom bunk and David and Chris slept in the top bunk. 'Cause we only lived in a three bedroom house and there were eight of us. But it was fun, we were real little.

I might be closest to Jordan, but I'm most *like* my sister Sharon. We both like stuff organized, and we can both be a little moody sometimes.

The whole family has always been real close. So it's kinda hard now when I'm not home a lot. Even with my mom's parents, Grandma Pearl and Grandpa Floyd Putman, I was always real close to them. They live in Canada, but they vacation in Florida during the winters. I told them, "I want to buy you guys a house in Florida." And my grandfather kept saying "No. We love you and you don't owe us anything." I think he's just a proud grandfather. So I just told him, "Listen, I'm buying the house in Florida whether you like it or not." And he was just so happy, there were tears in his eyes and everything. Made me feel so good. Like I said, we're all real close.

THE BIG VICTORIAN HOUSE

When I was four-and-a-half, we moved to this humongous house in Dorchester. When we first moved in, there were three different families still living there. On the first floor was an older couple from whom we bought the house. And on the second floor there was a teacher, who turned out to be David's and my teacher in middle school later on. And then on the third floor there were these newlyweds. When we moved in, we always used to go up to their floor, 'cause they were nice and gave us strawberry ice cream and stuff like that.

Some of the people in the house didn't move out right away when we moved in, so our family stayed on the first floor. It was weird—my brother and I used to sleep in the dining room. But eventually, all the other families moved out. We kids kept switching rooms. I've been in every single room in that house, I think.

THE GAMES I USED TO PLAY

My aunt always tells me I used to walk around the house and just tap people's shoulders. And she said I always whispered, I never spoke. But I had a lot of friends. When we were growing up, our neighbors on one side had, like, nine kids and our other neighbors had nine kids, and there were three kids behind us. We had fun. There's a hill behind our

street, and we used to build scooters and go-carts. And then in the wintertime, we used to turn on the fire hydrant and let the water freeze over, and we'd go sledding down the hill.

We built a tree fort, we always had parties in there. And we had an old Victorian carriage house in the yard, with a hayloft. We used to put on plays, and on Friday nights we'd have dances and stuff. We used to turn out the lights—it would be pitch dark in there—and we'd tell spooky stories and everything, and we'd all get scared. I remember one time, we'd heard about this girl in the neighborhood going around with a knife, and everybody was trying to get under the hay, because we'd scared ourselves into believing that the girl with the knife was coming!

I was always scared of the dark. I hate it when it's pitch dark—even now I sleep with the bathroom light on—so it was real spooky. And I was always afraid of monsters and stuff like that.

Then sometimes at nights we'd all stay in, watching TV. We used to like *The Brady Bunch*. I always watched *The Brady Bunch*. And *The Monkees* and *The Partridge Family* and *Donny and Marie*, mostly everything with music.

I was into sports too, but not as much as Jordan. I did soccer in school, and I did hockey when I was real little. It was crazy, with Jordan and me on the same team. We used to wake up at five in the morning to be there at six!

Even though we lived in the city, our house and property was so large that I always had lots of pets. I had a big yard and we had the carriage house, so I always had chickens, goats, pigs, rabbits, even a pony. You name it, we had it. When I was in about the fifth grade, I

TOP LEFT:
Christmas 1970, with my sister Allison (courtesy Marlene Putman)

TOP RIGHT:
1½ years old, at Grandma and Grandpa Putman's summer cottage in Canada (courtesy Marlene Putman)

BOTTOM RIGHT:
The brothers in their Canadian Maple Leaf plaid suits that Grandma Putman gave us (courtesy Marlene Putman)

started liking ducks, so I told my mother I wanted to get some. She took me to this farm, and we bought these five little teeny, teeny ducks. They were so small. I brought them home and kept them in my bedroom, in a box under a sink in my room. They used to just sit there. When they started getting bigger, I put them in my bathtub and let 'em swim around. They got so big that I built, like, a tub and lined it with plastic, and I put 'em outside. I had them for a year, but then I felt that this wasn't the right atmosphere for them, so I gave them to a friend of mine who had a pond.

FOSTER BROTHERS & SISTERS

My mom worked as a social worker—she's about to get her degree in psychology; she just has a little more to go—and she worked for an agency when we were growing up. And ever since I was very little, we always had foster brothers and sisters in the house. They were mostly older than me, teenagers from thirteen to eighteen. I think my real older sisters may not have liked it that much, but Jordan and I loved it. They used to take us bowling. And at that time there was another group home down the block where some of them lived with a group leader, and we'd get to go over there on Friday nights and stay up with the older kids. It was good.

Mostly these were kids who weren't getting along with their parents, who had problems. It was like a revolving door, with kids coming in and going out all the time. But even to this day, there's a few I still consider my sisters and brothers, a few I'm still in contact with. It was really a good growing experience. When I look back at it, it just taught me to understand people more, when they would talk about this and that, their experiences and other stuff.

There's some things I remember we did as a family, just the eight of us. Every summer, we'd pile into this Volkswagen bus that we had and drive up to my grandparents' cottage on Lake Erie. My Grandfather Putman built it when he was younger. We'd also go up to my father's sister's farm in Canada.

For a while we all had dinners together. My mom had a lot of mouths to feed. We had celebrations for each one's birthday, with cake and presents.

A WORKING KID

I started working probably when I was ten years old. I used to sell stuff door-to-door out of a catalogue; I'd go around the neighborhood. Then, when I was twelve years old, I got my first after-school job, working at

TOP:
My 2nd birthday! (courtesy Marlene Putman)

MIDDLE:
With Jordan; he's 3, I'm 4½ (courtesy Marlene Putman)

BOTTOM:
My family in January 1973 (courtesy Marlene Putman)

Burger King, because my sisters were managers there. I cooked and did everything. Sometimes, I'd stay real late, cleaning and stuff. I broke a lot of rules, 'cause I wasn't supposed to be doing all that at twelve years old, but I did.

I worked in a department store for a while and then I worked at a restaurant, but it didn't really have too much business. I started out as a busboy, along with the cook's brother, and then the cook started teaching us. When he left, I got to be the head cook. Shows you how much business they had! I cooked everything—steaks, hamburgers, spaghetti. Everybody thinks to cook in a restaurant is hard, but it's already made up, you just have to put it together.

That restaurant finally closed down, and other people bought it and turned it into a real nice Italian restaurant. They asked me to work there, and I did, but not as a cook. I was washing dishes there, and then I was a busboy and I cleared tables and stuff. But since it was such a real high-class restaurant by then, I was making great money in tips. The tips were like crazy! So I worked there four or five days a week. On Saturdays and Sundays I'd work, like, twelve hours straight. I saved a lot of money.

That was real important to me in those days, to have money so I could be independent and buy things for myself. I remember, my mother was always trying to buy me stuff, but I'd always rather get it for myself.

All this time I think my parents were proud of me. They weren't strict, they were pretty liberal. I mean, they got their point across, but they weren't strict about it. It's not like they ever grounded me or anything, but just growing up with them, you knew what was right and

TOP LEFT:
September 1972 with Great-Grandmother Putman and brothers and sisters (courtesy Marlene Putman)

TOP RIGHT:
I've always loved horses (courtesy Marlene Putman)

BOTTOM:
With one of my cousins (courtesy Marlene Putman)

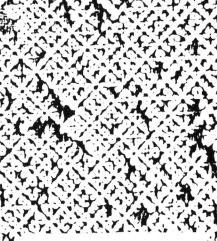

> **I started working when I was ten years old. I used to sell stuff door-to-door out of a catalogue; I'd go around the neighborhood. Then, when I was twelve years old, I got my first after-school job, working at Burger King.**

what was wrong. So we never really got into any trouble. I don't think I was spoiled, but if there was something I wanted to do, if there was a good reason for it, they would let me do it.

Most of the time, I felt close to my mother. I think everyone's closer with their mother. But I did a lot of stuff with my dad. Since my dad was a carpenter (as well as a minister) we built rabbit cages together. One time he built me this big rabbit cage, like eight feet long. It was cool. I had twenty-two rabbits. It was fun. Sometimes I went to work with my dad and did a lot of building with him. So I think that's why I like building so much.

THE CHURCH CHOIR

As a family, we went to church every week. I started singing in the choir at seven years old. Our choirmaster was Herb Peterson. I think he's been one of the biggest influences for me in music. It was just so much fun. We used to go on Wednesdays and Fridays and have choir rehearsal, and then on Sunday mornings we'd sing.

Herb was also the director at Camp St. Augustine which was our church camp, and all of us in the choir went there for several weeks every summer. It was run by the order of monks who were associated with our church. Aside from religious services, we did arts and crafts, music and went swimming. The camp was located in Foxboro, Massachusetts, not too far from where we lived. It's funny, because that's where Sullivan Stadium is, and that's one of the places we're playing on our Magic Summer tour this year.

I was real, real close to Herb. He was like my dad. He let me be a junior counselor at the camp when I was only fifteen. Herb was just always inspirational, someone I could always talk to.

He taught me a lot about music, mostly vocal stuff. I took piano lessons when I was real little, but it wasn't with him. And then in school I took music lessons, but with Herb it was mostly singing lessons. Herb taught me lots of vocal techniques that I still use today. I liked to sing, but Jordan was the one who was always singing around the house, everywhere he went, singing, singing, singing. He's still like that.

In the choir we sang only church music. I think it was real good to learn that type of music, because it was like . . . you know how the English Boys' Choirs sing? They're real strict about everything. We used to sing songs in Latin, and it was an English church, so they were always real strict about pronunciation. And we knew what the words meant, because they were from the Bible. Being in the church choir was probably one of the greatest experiences of my life, now that I look back on it.

Jonathan

ONE DAY I'LL BE A STAR . . . MAYBE

I admit that I used to dream about becoming famous. I know I used to run around the house with a microphone and stuff, and sing into the mirror. I think it's every kid's dream. When I was younger, I always knew I was gonna do something that was gonna make an impact. I always told my mother and father that. I told them I was gonna be famous. I just knew I was gonna do it at a young age. And then when this opportunity came along, to sing professionally and do all this, I was just like . . . "Oh! This is good. This is what I always wanted." But it's still kind of weird. I still have to pinch myself, saying, "Here I am, it happened."

Aside from church music, I listened to all kinds of music growing up. You name it, we had it. One of my sisters was into The Who—well, both of them were, really. They were into all types of groups. My brother used to like disco music, the Bee Gees and all that. They played a lot of everything, so I was really exposed to all different kinds of music.

SCHOOL DAYS

My older brothers and sisters were bused to the Trotter School for elementary, and that's where I went too. I might have met Danny Wood on the bus, but the truth is, I don't remember when we met. Danny's older sisters were friends with my sisters, and since everyone went to Trotter, it was like everybody always knew each other. Same with Donnie's family.

I wasn't in any classes with Donnie and Danny, I was usually across the hall from them since they were a grade lower. I never hung out with Danny in school, and I didn't really hang out with Donnie until fifth or sixth grade. Then, in seventh and eighth grade, I left for another school. It was actually Donnie's older brother Bobbo who was in my grade, so I hung around more with him. But I remember that Donnie was crazy, like he is today. In school he was always getting into trouble, but not bad trouble. And we'd all be sent to the principal—everybody was so scared of her. Miss Jackson was her name.

I think I always got good grades in school. I liked school when I was a kid. I always did good projects. Science was my favorite subject. I was in the chorus at Trotter and that was cool. We were always doing musicals, plays. We did *Winnie the Pooh*, and I was Christopher Robin. Jordan did a lot of stuff, too—he was Charlie from *Charlie and the Chocolate Factory*. Then he was in *Othello*, he was in a professional opera in Boston, when he was just a small little thing.

While Jordan was doing that, I was in the Boston Ballet for a while,

FROM TOP:

Summer 1986 (courtesy Marlene Putman)

Seven years old (courtesy Marlene Putman)

Eight years old (courtesy Marlene Putman)

Twelve years old (courtesy Marlene Putman)

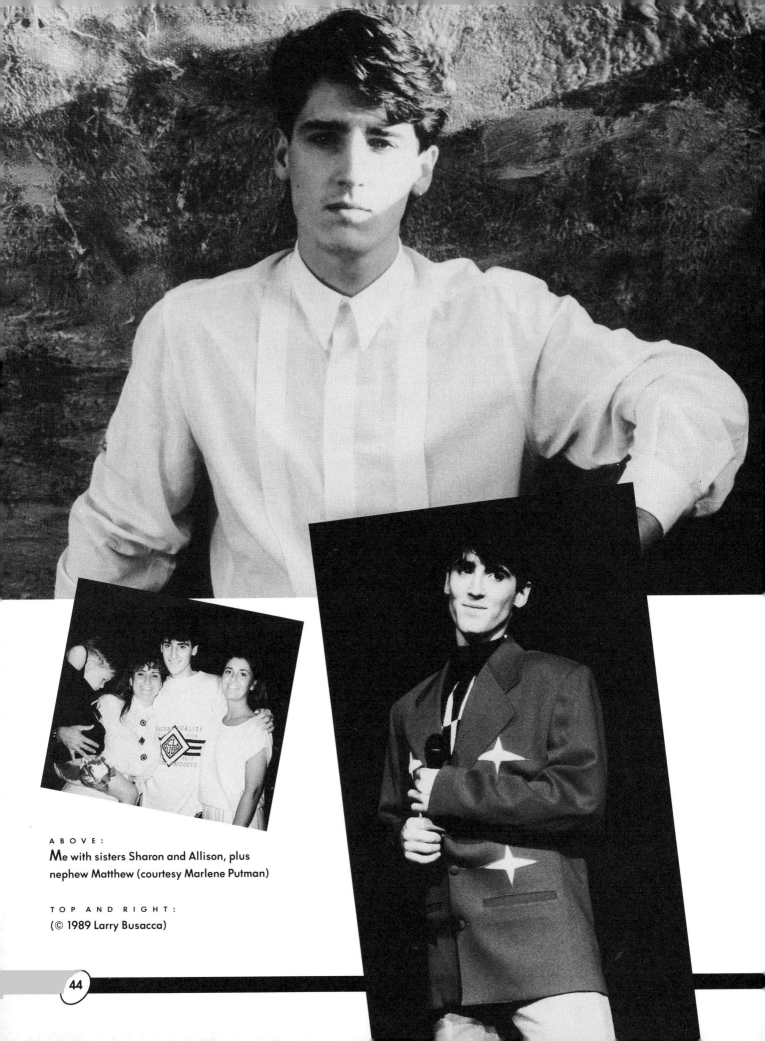

ABOVE:
Me with sisters Sharon and Allison, plus
nephew Matthew (courtesy Marlene Putman)

TOP AND RIGHT:
(© 1989 Larry Busacca)

in fifth grade. There was this kid in the chorus at Trotter who took dance lessons, and I remember one day seeing him dance and saying, "Man, that kid can dance!" I said I wanted to do that, so since my mother and his mother were good friends, I got to sign up. But within a week, they took me out of the class I was in and put me with all these grown-up people. They did it because they thought I was good, but it felt so weird. First I was in a class with kids my own age, and then all of a sudden I ended up with all these grown-ups. I had a part in *The Nutcracker*, but I was scared and so I didn't stay in it very long.

One more thing I remember about elementary school—that's where I started liking girls. I had my first crush in the third grade. There was this girl named Delores, I don't remember her last name. She used to live two houses down from where the school playground ended. And when she wasn't in school, during recess, I'd always kick the ball down the street so I could run down to her house and see if she was on the porch or something.

In the sixth grade, Donnie and I liked this one girl, the same girl. Her name was Thea Richardson. I just thought she was incredible. Donnie thought the same way. We used to sneak down to the girls' bathroom during lunch, me and Donnie and this girl Thea, and we'd be sitting there, talking away.

For middle school, I went to the Thayer Academy. I started out in sixth grade at the public school, which was Wheatley, where Donnie and Danny went, but Jordan and I got scholarships to Thayer, which was private. It was in the suburbs, and they were trying to get city kids to come there. Another kid who grew up with us and who was in the choir went there, and he told us about it. He was older and in the high school division at Thayer, and his dad drove us there every day. I wish I could have stayed there. The education I got in that school in the two years I was there was incredible. It was so much fun. I enjoyed science and stuff. The teachers were like professors, it was like going to college, and it was rough! I know for the first year, I tried so hard, but I was only getting C's and D's. I wasn't real prepared for it, but I was learning so much.

The kids were different at Thayer than they were at Trotter. At Trotter it was racially mixed, and at Thayer it was mostly wealthy white kids. They were into designer jeans, and Jordan and I didn't wear that stuff, but I think because we were the tough city kids, they were intimidated by us at first. But a majority of kids liked us and thought it was cool—here were these city dudes comin' in. But it took a while for other kids to come around. But eventually, we were, like, *the* two kids at the school.

For high school, things got a little messed up. I started at English

> " Elementary school—that's when I first started liking girls. I had my first crush in the third grade... She used to live two houses down from where the school playground ended... I'd always kick the ball down the street so I could run down to her house and see if she was on the porch or something. "

High, and then when my parents got divorced, I left school for a while. I went to night school to catch up, a private night school where you could do that.

When I was ready to go back to public high school, they suddenly said they wouldn't accept the work I'd done in night school, but they did work it out where I could graduate—or I would have, anyway—a year later than most of my class. But then the group came along. The school didn't want to give me any credit for being on the road and working with a tutor and stuff, so it got all complicated. But I am working with a tutor now, the same one that Joe works with. And my grades are really good, so I will be graduating.

TEEN YEARS

Aside from weird things with school, I didn't really go through a wild period as a teenager. It was strange because when I was twelve, I was working around eighteen- and nineteen-year-olds. And being around a lot of grown-up people, I think I was always beyond my age. 'Cause when I was twelve, I was doing the type of things teenagers do when they're older, hanging out and stuff. And then when *I* got to be older, Jordan would say, "What's wrong with you? Why don't you want to go to the clubs" and "why don't you want to do this and that?" And I always told him, "I did all that already." I did stuff like going to parties and staying out all night, sleeping at my friend's house. My mother always knew about it. I wasn't sneaking behind her back.

And before I was a teenager, I was riding the subways by myself, back and forth, going shopping downtown. Now I look at little kids on the subways and think, "They're too young to be doing this."

Yeah, I was a street kid, but it's not like what everyone thinks of when they hear "street kid." They think about us being vandals and hoodlums, but we weren't. We weren't any different from any other city kids. Kids who live out in the suburbs, they have their dads' cars, but we were street kids 'cause we were riding the subways and playing baseball in vacant lots.

The worst thing for me when I was a teenager, I guess, was when my parents got divorced. I was like fifteen or something. Not that it was that big a shock. Growing up, I always asked my parents, "Are you guys gonna get divorced?" I mean, my mom and dad didn't fight all that much, just about little things like all parents do. But I think they just came from such different backgrounds and wanted different things, that they probably weren't real happy together. I think maybe my fa-

ther wanted to get divorced all along, but he knew he had kids and re-sponsibilities and he had to do his part.

It was weird the way he went about telling us—he only told three of us. I think *I* told Jordan. It was around Christmas, and there was so much left unresolved and so many weird feelings and all. Because my mother's a social worker, we talked through a lot of stuff with her—we've always been very open with her—and we found out a lot of stuff we didn't know. And that's helped. But to this day, I'm still not really sure what happened.

But because we're famous, the tabloids have made this huge gigantic mess out of it all, and it's really not that big a deal. There are millions of other kids in America whose parents are divorced. I'm just like any of them.

The whole rest of the family has stayed really close. My mom and brothers fly out to see me when I'm on the road, and my sisters help run the fan club. It's nice to keep it all in the family.

ABOVE:
The entire family made it to the party for Grandpa and Grandma Putman's 50th wedding anniversary! Back row: Jonathan, cousin Nathan, brother David, cousin Aaron, Uncle Wayne, brother Christopher, Jordan, Uncle Gary. Front row: cousin Kim, cousin Rachel, sister Sharon, Aunt Lynda, Grandpa Putman, Grandma Putman, our mother Marlene, sister Allison, and Aunt Ann. In front: niece Alicia and nephew Matthew. (courtesy Marlene Putman)

OPPOSITE:
(courtesy Marlene Putman)

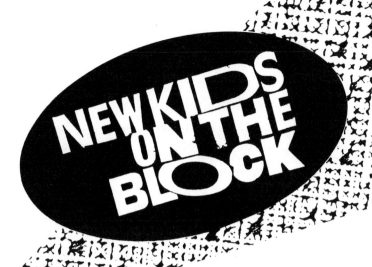

DANNY
WOOD

I've lived in the Dorchester section of Boston my whole life. I was born there at St. Margaret's Hospital on May 14, 1969, and I was the fourth child in my family. My parents are Daniel Joseph and Elizabeth—everybody calls my mom Betty. I was named Daniel William, after my dad and my grandfather. I'm not a "Jr.," because my dad and I have different middle names. My older sisters are Bethany, Melissa, and Pamela. A few years after me, my brother Brett was born and then one year later, my little sister Rachel.

Our first house was a three-decker. In Boston, that's a three family. But there wasn't much room. My father's a mailman and my mother wasn't working back then, because she was having babies. So we were kind of struggling then.

When I was five, my father bought another house, just down the street from our first one. It was bigger, but I never had my own room or anything. I didn't get my own room until about a year

ago! That was after my sister got married and moved out. Now, actually, I own the house; I bought it from my parents. We're all still going to live there together, but we're re-doing the attic, raising the roof and widening it. And it's going to be a whole apartment for me.

But when I was growing up, I always shared with Brett. My brother and I are pretty close. We always had bunk beds. And I just remember all the time before we'd go to bed, we would just always talk, about anything. Growing up, he always tried to do the things that I would do. Up until a certain point, anyway. Up until he got into high school. That's when he stopped emulating me. But before that it would be like, I'd join the track team, he'd join the track team. I would do breakdancing, he asked me to teach him to breakdance. But he's his own person now.

Even though we had such a large family, I never felt crowded or anything, and I never felt I wasn't getting enough attention. I was close to all my sisters and my brother, and my parents always treated everyone equally. The major thing that they stressed for all of us was education, that we did well in school. They really kept on us about that.

FRIENDS & FUN

I was a real adventurous kid. And really into girls when I was little. I remember being in kindergarten and liking girls. I had a crush on this girl named Beth. I'll never forget that—I don't know why. I was too shy to do anything about it, though. She still lives up the street from me—but I don't have a crush on her anymore.

I was a mischievous kid, and I had a lot of friends, in my neighborhood and in school. I probably had more friends as a little kid than I did when I got into high school. When you're little, you accept everyone, you don't realize what they're all about. But when I got older, I saw that some of the people I was friends with were prejudiced, and I stopped being friends with them. When I was small, I didn't know that.

We used to play cops and robbers, and hide and seek. We played in the streets 'cause it was a small neighborhood. There always seemed to be a lot of kids around, kids everywhere. Now I drive around my neighborhood, and there don't seem to be as many kids. But when I was growing up, it was fun.

I played sports with my friends, nothing real organized. I would play whatever everyone else was playing. You know, a lot of baseball during the summer and, later on, in seventh and eighth grade, basketball. We used to set up a milk crate and nail it to a tree. Shoot the basketball through that. Actually, it wasn't usually a basketball, more like some kind of volleyball or something—it was just kind of a makeshift game.

My main sport was track. I ran track for four or five years, all year round. In the spring it was outdoors and in the winter, we'd do some indoor meets and a lot of cross-country races. I was kind of fast. I used to run everything from the 100 meter dash to the mile. I did six-mile road races too. So I was pretty fast, I guess. For about four years in a row, I was in the top five. And I came in third in different events for four straight years. I won something like twenty-five trophies. There are lots of ribbons and medals and stuff somewhere in my room.

Running track was real important to me for a long time, all the way up through my early teen years. But then I lost interest, because, you know, all you do is run. You just run. And also, I was running in a lot of pain. I had bad knees for a while—I have good knees now—but back then I was in pain a lot, and it just wasn't enjoyable after a while. So I quit. And I'm really not the type to quit anything. But I knew I had reached my plateau. I wasn't going any further.

THE THINGS WE DID TOGETHER

We were a pretty tight family. We'd always have Sunday dinner with my grandparents on my father's side. They lived close by. Christmases were always special. Every year, we used to have this huge Christmas party where everyone would come from both sides of the family. I have great memories, but the best Christmas ever was last year, because I could really do a lot more for my family. I was able to give my parents a twelve-day trip to Hawaii for their winter vacation and I gave all my sisters nice jewelry—gold rope chains and things like that. And I bought my brother a car. So it was a real special Christmas.

Birthdays were big events in my family too. When we were little, we'd have all the neighborhood kids there. But as we got older, it would be basically family and a few friends, maybe a girlfriend if I had one at the time. I don't have one special birthday that stands out, just a warm feeling of remembering that my family and friends cared about me and took the time to do things for me.

Every summer we'd go on vacation, my whole family. We would always take a trip. We went to Hersheypark once and one time we flew to Florida. That was the furthest we went. The most fun we had were the summers we spent in Bryant Pond, Maine, because we would be with all our cousins. We'd have a trailer and it was like having a whole community all for ourselves. We'd swim in the lake, build birdhouses out of wood, sing around the campfire, and toast marshmallows. We liked going to New Hampshire, too. Now my parents own a condominium in New Hampshire, so everyone goes there a lot. But I haven't had a chance to go yet.

The other thing we'd do together, every Sunday, was go to church, up

TOP:
Just a party kind of guy, May 1972 (courtesy Betty Wood)

MIDDLE:
Almost two years old—me and my sisters (courtesy Betty Wood)

BOTTOM:
Me and my sisters, July 1972 (courtesy Betty Wood)

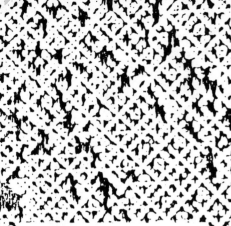

> **The most fun we had were the summers we spent in Bryant Pond, Maine, because we would be with all our cousins...We'd swim in the lake, build birdhouses out of wood, sing around the campfire, and toast marshmallows.**

until I was probably seventeen or so. We can't do that as a family much anymore, but it was good to have that as a kid. Now, I believe in God and I talk to Him.

OFF TO SCHOOL

My whole family—all my sisters, my brother and I—went to the same school, the William Monroe Trotter Elementary School. When we started, that's when busing started in Boston. Every morning, we'd get on the school bus. The school was in Roxbury, which is the next neighborhood over. It was only three miles away, but it took twenty minutes to get there, because we picked up a lot of kids along the way.

We were the minority there. There were more black kids and Puerto Rican kids and Chinese kids than white kids. We didn't care, to us it didn't matter. And I don't think my parents were worried about it or anything, because my mother used to work for the Boston School Committee, and both my parents were always very involved in the school system. They knew all the parents of the other kids, and all the teachers too.

I probably didn't realize it then, but now I would say that going there made us all better people. All six of us. We learned about other people, and we learned not to judge people by the color of their skin or anything. The only problem I ever had with that was when I got a little older and I realized that some people in my neighborhood—not at school—*were* prejudiced. And they didn't like me anymore, because I had friends of all backgrounds. So when I was home, I began keeping to myself more, in my house. I wouldn't hang in my neighborhood. I would hang in other places, where I had real friends, not people who would judge me by the people I hung around with.

Donnie was bused to the same school and that's where I first met him, even though my sisters knew his brothers. My sister Melissa even went out with his brother Paul for a little while. Donnie and I weren't real tight in elementary school, though. I remember seeing Donnie and just saying to him, you know, "What's up?" We would talk in school—we were in the same grade—but not outside of school. Donnie had this reputation as the "wild one," but he wasn't really a troublemaker—he never started any trouble with me.

The Trotter School is where I met Jordan and Jon. I wasn't really friends with them either at that time; I just remember having an impression of Jon as this real ladies' man. Even in elementary school, he would always have girls around him.

MERRY CHRISTMAS

The Woods

TOP LEFT:
Me in kindergarten (courtesy Betty Wood)

BOTTOM LEFT:
Three years old (courtesy Betty Wood)

TOP RIGHT:
I'm five, Brett is two (courtesy Betty Wood)

BOTTOM RIGHT:
Merry Christmas 1972! (courtesy Betty Wood)

> " I've read where people have called us 'street kids,' but I don't think that's fair to say about any of us...I would breakdance and go to dances and clubs and parties, but I would never get into bad things like hanging out on the corner all day. "

THE SCHOOL CHORUS

I actually first met the Knights because we were in chorus together at Trotter. We all had to try out and sing in front of the teacher. It was kind of scary, because I never thought I had a good voice, but I didn't have to sing too much. A funny thing is that Donnie tried out too, and he didn't make it. This was like in the fourth or fifth grade, so I still didn't know him very well, but it's funny looking back on it now.

I was an alto in the chorus. Jordan and Jon were sopranos—they had higher voices. We would do concerts at school, and once in a while we'd go to high schools and City Hall and perform, and do different things like that. I remember one time we did a musical, and we all danced around. I liked doing things like that. I remember I was in *Peter Pan* and I was one of the Lost Boys. I played Slightly Soiled.

But what I liked best about being in the chorus was the applause. I used to *really* love that.

I would sometimes dream about becoming famous, not so much as a singer exactly, but as something in show business. Everyone dreams about that, but I was the kind of kid who liked to go out there and do things, but *not* want to be the center of attention. I'm still that way. Even when I'm out on stage and doing a song, I don't feel that *I'm* the center of attention, that this is *my* time. It's not like, "Hey, everyone's looking at me, let me get busy!" I'm just part of the team, trying to do the best I can do.

ON TO MIDDLE SCHOOL

For middle school, I went to the Phyllis Wheatley School. That was pretty much the same, being bused and very mixed racially. Like in elementary school, I was always a good student, did my work. My favorite subject in middle school was English, mainly because of my teacher, Mr. Millman. It's funny, because I remember him being kind of strict and not everyone liked him. But he was probably one of the best teachers I ever had. He wouldn't just make us do our work out of a textbook—he would get into telling us stories and his stories would be so incredible. I loved all those stories, and I really learned a lot from him.

It was in seventh grade that Donnie and I became friends, really hanging out. That's when we started doing some rap together, though I'm not really a rapper. I can do it, I like to, but it was really Donnie's thing more than mine. He would write routines, and we would do them together at a party or at school. He got me into that.

Donnie was always good in school. He was adventurous and a ham

Who's the big one in the middle? (courtesy Betty Wood)

and into having fun, but he was always a smart student. He was smarter than me. His grades might not have been the best, but I think he's smarter. He was just a comedian and more into having adventures than I was. I would always just do my work.

That wasn't only because my parents were on top of me about my grades. I think at a certain point you're either going to listen to your parents or not listen to them. You just become your own person. Once I got into the upper grades, I think I became my own person, and I just knew that doing well in school was the right thing to do.

I would have to say that when I was a young teenager, my parents were pretty strict. They're a lot more lenient now with my brother and sister. My mother would say things like "Wait 'til your father gets home," and up until the time I was seventeen I was pretty scared of him. We used to call him "The Voice of Authority," because the way he punished us was mainly by yelling real loud. We'd stand there blank-faced while he reprimanded us.

I can't complain, because, basically, as a teenager I could do what I wanted to. Sometimes I couldn't stay out as late as I wanted to or as my friends could. But the only real trouble I got into with my parents when I was younger was when they would go away and I would have friends over without telling them. That was something my sister Melissa and I used to get into trouble for. After Bethany and Pamela moved out, we were occasionally left in charge of Brett and Rachel, and we'd kinda be in cahoots with each other. We'd both invite our

Danny's dad and mom with his niece Daniela (photo by Danny Wood)

friends over and it was like, "I won't tell on you if you don't tell on me." And then we'd have to quickly clean up before our parents got home. They were really neat and would know right away if one small thing was out of place.

One thing we always had to do was our chores. Every Sunday we would have to clean up our rooms. Vacuum them, dust them, and then help my mother downstairs. It wasn't too bad. I used to have to wash the front stairs. That was my job. We had fireplaces and a wood-burning stove that my father would get wood for. Except he would get it all in one big chunk, not cut up. So he would be out there cutting it all day, and I remember my brother and I would always have to stack the wood. That would be a whole-day thing. I don't regret doing it, but I used to resent it sometimes—just because a lot of times it was on the weekend and I'd rather be doing things with my friends.

BREAKING INTO DANCING

There was always music in my house while I was growing up. I always listened to the radio. My older sisters used to like pop music, like the Bay City Rollers. I used to laugh at them for that—I used to think that kind of music really stunk. I liked R&B and rap. Back as far as fifth grade, I would listen to Sister Sledge, the SOS band, groups like that. I never bought any records or tapes or anything, just used to listen to the radio. I never went to any concerts either when I was younger. I think my first one was Luther Vandross, and by that time I was already in New Kids, *giving* concerts!

Dancing was really my main thing, though, more than singing or rapping. I remember when I was in the fifth grade and there was this dance out. I can't remember the name of it. I just remember, I would dance and I'd be the only white kid dancing. When breakdancing started, I got right into that, and I'd be the only white kid breakdancing.

I would just watch people and pick up the moves. No one ever sat down and taught me. But I got into it really heavy, not just at school and with my friends, but even right in my driveway at home. I'd put down a rug and some linoleum—my little sister would do it too—and practice my moves. My mother would always get so nervous watching us. She'd say, "Watch your head! Watch your head!" I never hurt my head, but I did have some nasty bruises on my knees from doing that.

I joined this breakdancing group, Rock Against Racism, which was funded through charitable donations. All different people—white kids, black kids, Spanish kids—came together and we would perform

With one of my awards for track (courtesy Betty Wood)

throughout Boston on different holidays, like Martin Luther King Day. I liked that a lot. I wasn't the best or the most outstanding, but I was good and I was recognized for being good—and I was part of a team.

THE "DO-GOOD WOOD" STREET KID

Another "team" I was part of wasn't a music group. It was the Kool Aid Bunch. It was like a posse. I forget who came up with the name, but it included me, Donnie, our friends Elliot, David, Lonnie, and a few others. And we would always be together and also go on adventures, looking for fun. We hung out together, on the streets, on the subway after school, whatever.

I've read where people have called us "street kids," but I don't think that's fair to say about any of us. What *is* a street kid? I would breakdance and go to dances and clubs and parties, but I would never get into bad things like hanging out on the corner all day. I didn't really like doing that. I would just be into the fun things, and not, like, hanging out and getting into drugs, things like that.

I would always keep doing well in school, no matter what I was doing on the outside. I knew what was going on around me and people would offer me drugs. There'd be bad things happening around me. But I was always into the good and positive things. They used to call me "Do-Good Wood."

HANGIN' IN HIGH SCHOOL

I went to Copley Square High School—actually, its full name was The Copley Square School of International Studies. But now it has a different name. Copley was right in the heart of downtown Boston and it was an exciting place to be. There was no more busing by that time—not for high school kids anyway—so to get there, we took the subway. Like the other schools I went to, it was pretty mixed. We were still the minority.

Being popular wasn't really a big thing with me; I didn't care all that much. But high school was when I finally overcame my shyness with girls. I always liked girls, but up until high school I was kind of shy around them, scared to talk to them. But then I started getting more confident and talking to whole bunches of girls!

High school was pretty cool to me. Just waking up in the morning was a hassle. Especially in my senior year, 'cause by then, I pretty much had all the points I needed to graduate. I was finished with all my requirements by then, and I was just taking options. So who wanted to get up for that?

My grades in high school were really good—except for one. I had straight A's—and one F, because I refused to take a class with my Spanish teacher. I'd had him in ninth and tenth grade and I didn't learn anything from him. I felt, here I was in my fourth year of Spanish and I didn't know anything. So I decided I wasn't going to take it anymore.

That didn't stop me from getting a scholarship to college. I was offered scholarships to three colleges, including one for four years to Boston University, which I accepted. My SATs weren't that great, but my grades were. Actually, I think it was the essay that I did for the application form that got me in. I can't remember what I wrote, but my mom helped me with it.

COLLEGE & THE BIG DECISION

I started going to Boston University, and that was really the craziest time in my life. First of all, the work was very hard. I never really had to work that hard before; getting A's came easy to me. But at college, I had to read like four books at a time and do all these projects. I could have handled it, except that by that time, I was already with the group. New Kids started when I was in tenth grade, but because we weren't successful right off, I never had to miss school for it. But that first year in college we were in the recording studio working on *Hangin' Tough*. The thing was, I was engineering a lot of that album. I loved that, and I wanted to be in the studio every single second. So I wasn't concentrating on school as much as I would have—and I was getting C's and B's and maybe one D.

So I had a decision to make. I talked to my professors, and they really thought I should leave and do the group full-time. They said I could come back, that the scholarship would still be there. But it took a lot to convince my parents. They didn't like my decision at all, which was understandable. They insisted I get a job, and so I worked in a travel agency, delivering airline tickets. I did that for six months, until our first single broke and we got the tour with Tiffany.

SAYING I LOVE YOU

Right now, I probably feel the strongest sense of family that I ever have. Since I'm away all the time, I guess I've learned to appreciate my family more. Growing up, we never said things like "I love you" to each other. I always knew my parents loved me, but we just never said it. Now, I say it all the time. I've learned that you've got to let people know you love them, 'cause any time something can happen. I lost my grandfather, two of my uncles and my cousin—who was only twenty-four—all within two years' time, and it made me realize that you never know what's going to happen. So now, every time I talk to my mother or my father, I tell them I love them.

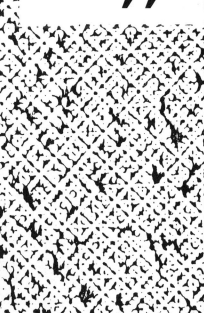

> " My main sport was track... I used to run everything from the hundred-meter dash to the mile...I won something like twenty-five trophies. "

Mary Alford with the Kids (photo by Stacey Woolf)

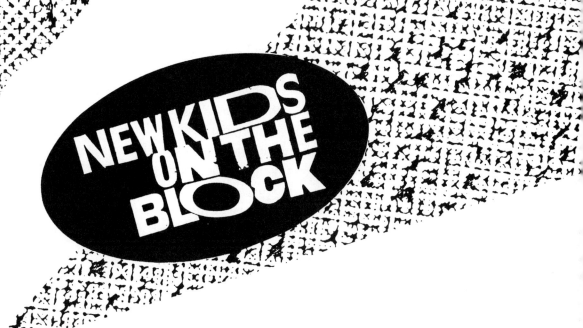

NEW KIDS ON THE BLOCK

GETTING TOGETHER

There's been all kinds of crazy stories about how we actually got together as a group. Here's the real one.

DONNIE'S STORY

A friend of mine named Gina Macucci told me that her neighbor, Mary Alford, who's a talent manager, was lookin' for kids to try out for a group. So I was thinking, all right, I'll do it, I'll do it, but I just never got around to doing it. Finally, Mary came to my house to pick me up to go to try out one day and I was busy. My father was yellin' at me to mow the lawn, so I had to mow the lawn. But Mary said, "I'll come back." She did come back and I got to go. That was in July of 1984.

My little brother Mark and I went together, and we met Maurice Starr. He's a singer and producer, who worked with New Edition,

Bobby Brown, and other groups. He was real famous, and I knew his name from the record albums I'd seen. Maurice and Mary were working together on this. The whole thing was their idea.

When I met Maurice, he had me sing, rap, dance. I wasn't the greatest singer, but he wasn't looking for the greatest singer for this group. I mean, if a great, great singer walked in, I don't think he would've had any more of a chance than I did, 'cause that's not what Maurice was looking for.

Right away, Maurice told me I made it. Mark made it too. They asked me to try and find some other kids. The truth is that they weren't auditioning a lot of kids—no more than twenty people tried out for New Kids On The Block.

So first I thought of Danny, and this is what's so incredible—Danny should never have been in the group, 'cause he didn't want to try out. I think he was scared to death to try out. I remember asking him and asking him and asking him, and he kept saying, "No, no, no." Mary Alford said, "Well, forget him, then. He doesn't want to do it, you can't make him do it." But he finally did and he made it.

Then Mary and I went out one day driving in the neighborhood looking for kids to ask to try out. I drove by Jordan's street. I hadn't seen him in three years and I said, "Yo, Jordan and Jonathan live on this street." I had to call five people to get Jordan's number. I asked him to try out and he did, and he brought Jonathan.

In the beginning, there was also Jamie Kelly. He was my buddy, he was sort of a rapper, we did a few rap tapes together for fun. He was real, real funny—he was crazy.

My brother Mark didn't stay in the group too long. He just wasn't into it. He was real young, under fifteen. He decided to drop out. I respect him for that because it took a lot for him to stand up and say, "No, that's not what I want to do." Everyone was probably pressuring him to stick with the group, saying, "You'll be rich, you'll do this, you'll do that, you'll be famous." So for him to stand up and say, "No, I don't want to do it" took a lot of character. He did it and I respect him for that. I hope he doesn't have any regrets about it now.

Jamie stayed longer, but he stopped showing up for rehearsals and he wasn't really into it, either. And his parents didn't want him in it, so after a while he dropped out too.

When I first told my mother about it, she didn't pay too much attention, 'cause I was always coming up with different schemes and she had no way of knowing what was going to pan out. I'd go to rehearsal, and she didn't really know what it was all about. Then one day I brought a tape home and played it for her. She was blown away. She said, "Who's that singing?" I said, "It's *me*, ma." From that moment on,

Mary Alford, with Donnie and his brother Bobbo (courtesy Alma Conroy)

she really got into it. She met Maurice, and after talking to him, she came away believing that we really were going to make it. She started coming to our rehearsals, and she got behind us 100 percent.

JORDAN'S STORY

At the time I heard about it, I was more or less just hanging in the streets with my friends, and breakdancing. One day, out of the blue, Donnie called me up. I hadn't talked to Donnie since elementary school. He asked me if I wanted to go audition for some group that was no game—it was for real, and it wasn't a small-time thing.

I really didn't know what to think, 'cause when I was a breakdancer, a lot of people used to approach me and tell me they were going to put me in a troupe, tell me I'd make all this money. But it was just a lot of talk. So I thought Donnie's thing might just be another one of those things. But I wanted to check it out, y'know. Donnie set up a date to take me to Maurice Starr's house.

Donnie called me in the first place because he knew all along that I was in church choir and I could sing. And he knew I was a good dancer. So he came to my house in the winter of 1984, took me to Maurice's house, and Maurice tried me out. He had everyone leave the room, and he had me sing "Be My Girl," the same song that's on our first album. He played it on the piano and said, "Sing this part here." And I sang the lines back to him. But all I really sang was one line, and he said, "All right. You're cool." That was it!

I don't know how I felt; it was still weird. I mean, Maurice was talking so *big* that it set my head twirlin', really. He was telling me, "You're gonna be rich, you're gonna be the biggest thing in America"—after he met me for only five minutes! I told him, "I don't care about all that. All I want is a scooter!" And he said, "Boy, you'll have a scooter for every day of the year."

> **It wasn't too long before I saw that Donnie and Danny were great guys. That's when I started feeling a part of it all, when we all clicked and hung together. They became my best friends.**
>
> **—JORDAN**

I went back home and told my mother about it, and she thought it was a fluke. But for some reason, Maurice hyped everything so bad, he really drove it into my brain that we were gonna be real big—and I believed him. It was just something about the way he said it. You could see the excitement in his eyes. I told my mother, and she didn't believe it either at first. But after checkin' Maurice out thoroughly and spending a long time straight-talking with him, *she* came away believing him too.

A couple of days later, Jonathan went to the studio to try out. The truth is that I didn't go to his audition. I wasn't there. I was into my friends, my own thing on the street, really. And I didn't want to be bothered, y'know. The real truth is that at first, I wasn't that into it,

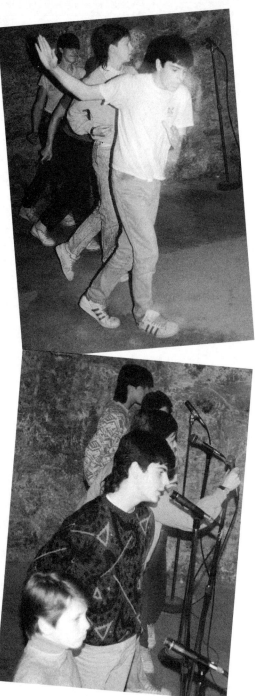

May 1986, rehearsing our moves in the garage (courtesy Marlene Putman)

May 1986, doing our thing (courtesy Marlene Putman)

Danny in NYNUK (courtesy Betty Wood)

because Donnie and Danny were so different than I was. They were so different from my friends, and I was thinking that all the time Maurice and Mary wanted us to put into this was time I'd have to be away from my people. It was a major commitment, but eventually, I made it.

It wasn't too long before I saw that Donnie and Danny were great guys. That's when I started feeling a part of it all, when we all clicked and hung together. They became my best friends.

DANNY'S STORY

Donnie had been telling me for a long time about this group. He'd been involved for several months, since the summer of 1984. It wasn't until the next January that the rest of us really got together. So he was in it the whole time, telling me—'cause we were in school together—"Come on, join this group, man. It's going to be dope." (That's our way of saying, great, or the best.) I told him, "No, man, I'm going to do this show"—I was in a breakdancing group called Rock Against Racism at the time, and I was doing shows with them—and this and that. I was going to clubs and going with girls and really just into breakdancing.

Donnie explained that it was a singing group, and I said, "Yo, I can't sing." And he said, "Neither can I, but once you get in, you gear yourself to sing." So it took him a while, but he finally convinced me to try out. So I tried out, and I had to sing, like, one line for Maurice. It was not a big deal. He wanted to see if we could hear what he was singing and sing it in the same key. Maurice likes to take people and bring their talent out. But Maurice was so jive, he said, "You guys are going to be bigger than the Beatles." I breakdanced for him, and he really liked that. He saw that I wasn't scared to get out there in front of people and do something I could do well.

Donnie was there, watching me audition. When it was over, he said, "Cool, you're in the group." Jordan had tried out earlier in the week, and he was in, and another kid named Jamie was already in. I think Jonathan and I tried out the same day. So that's how it started.

JONATHAN'S STORY

I was about sixteen. I know it was wintertime. Jordan had already been out to Maurice's studio before he even told me or my mother about it. One day when he came home, my mom said, "Where have you been?" He told her all about the audition and the group. At first my mom was skeptical, but after she checked Maurice out, she asked if they were looking for another kid, meaning me. She knew it would be something I'd be interested in doing too.

The next day, Mary picked me up and drove me to Maurice's. I'll never forget how I felt that day, or what he said to me. It wasn't really a big, formal audition. He asked me to sing, and my knees were shaking. All I could think of was, "This is my one chance, and what if I mess it up?" I was so nervous, I'm sure I sang really badly, but Maurice is the kind of person who can see through that stuff.

And when he told me I'd made the group, he said, "You're even handsomer than your brother."

I never really understood Maurice. He's real jive. He started right away putting all this positive stuff in our heads, making us believe this was gonna be great. If it hadn't worked out, it would have been really sad, because Maurice really got us all hyped up.

Maurice gave me the opportunity, but I thank God for the day Donnie drove by our block and thought about us for the group.

JOE'S STORY

I was this kid, y'know, only twelve. I was doing community theater and goin' to school. Mary Alford, who was our first manager with Maurice, was looking for a young kid for their group. They already had Donnie, Danny, Jordan, and Jonathan. There was this kid Jamie, but he had quit, so there was an opening. And Mary and Maurice decided they wanted a younger kid.

They had this idea that their group could be the new Osmond Brothers or the Jackson 5, and they were looking for someone with a high voice to be the "Donny Osmond" or the "Michael Jackson."

So Mary was calling around to all these schools in Boston and voice coaches, asking if they knew of any kids who could sing and dance. Finally, she made a connection, someone who knew me and said, "Oh, yeah, Joseph McIntyre. He's a kid you should see." But this person wouldn't give Mary my phone number and address, so she still couldn't find me. Then she heard that I sometimes played basketball at a community school, and that's where she found me.

She told me about the group, but at first I didn't want to go. It was all these Dorchester kids, and me and Dorchester seemed like worlds apart. Plus, I was happy with what I was doing, and I wasn't really looking to get into anything new.

The funny thing was, my sister had heard of the group. She'd gone to a show at a local club, and Nynuk—that was their name at the time—was the opening act for Lisa Lisa and the Cult Jam. And my sister liked them.

> " As the years went on, we had a million tour buses...We've gone through buses left and right, they were always breaking down. "
>
> —DANNY

I decided to go to the audition and told my mom about it. She wasn't too keen on the idea, but she didn't object too strongly. She just figured my dad would say no. For some reason, he didn't. So I went.

I remember it was June 1985. Mary picked me up in her car and drove me to Maurice's house, where I just tried out. I sang, and they liked me, and I got in.

The hardest part for me was meeting the others. They all knew each other, and they were older, and they didn't like me. I came in replacing Donnie's friend, which they understood, but still there was this resentment. And I took over a lot of the leads right away, which Jordan really wanted to do. He never said anything at the time, but years later he admitted he was jealous.

Donnie was the one who picked on me the most. And Jordan was his sidekick. Danny kept to himself. He didn't really bother me or anything like that. He would laugh at their jokes, though. They would joke and tease me about anything, anything at all. I can't remember exactly what they would say, except for this one thing. Because I had stage experience, I was able to pick up the choreography right away; I was usually pretty fast. This one time, though, I didn't get it right off, it took me a while, so they started calling me "Slow Joe."

It was rough for me, really rough. I used to go home in Mary's car and just cry. It was a hard time. I remember several times I would go home crying.

It was rough at home too. This new helter-skelter schedule I was suddenly on—with rehearsals being called at the last minute, or cancelled at the last minute—drove my mother nuts. She's very orderly and didn't like the family routine being constantly disrupted.

I thought about quitting all the time. I'm not really sure why I didn't. No one was pressuring me. I could have quit just like that. I think partly it was Mary. She was one reason I stayed. She taught me a lot and convinced me it would get better, that I should stay. But the main reason, I guess, was the shows we were starting to do. It was kind of like signing up for a show at the community theater—whether you loved or hated the rehearsals, you stayed for opening night. You didn't quit. And once I got up there on stage, I loved it. Hearing the applause has always made everything worth it.

REMEMBERING THE EARLY DAYS

Lots of people still think of us as an "overnight sensation," five kids who hit the limelight in 1989 and made it big right away. Nothing could be further from the truth. From the summer of 1985, when we were all finally together as a group, until *Hangin' Tough* hit in 1989, we paid our dues, all right.

For four years we worked really hard and had our share of failures before we got successful. But there were fun times, too, in those good old "uncomplicated" days. Here are some of our memories.

Jonathan:

Pretty much as soon as we were together, we signed up with Mary and Maurice. Since we were young, our parents had to be involved, and that was cool too. But I don't think we realized what we were in for.

Donnie:

Dick Scott is someone who was also there with us and for us right from the start. Dick is Maurice's manager and was on hand to consult with and advise us. That was important, because he had a lot of big-time experience in the music business, and that helped us a lot. In fact, in about a year, Dick became our official manager.

Jordan:

Mary worked us really hard, from 5:30 to 9 P.M. every day after school, five days a week. It was *hard*. We'd come home beat tired, and we'd have to go to school the next day. For me, the biggest problem with all of it was that it took me away from my friends and everything I was doing.

Donnie:

We started going to singing classes, and then into the studio.

Joe:

Maurice taught us his music and helped me learn to stylize my singing. His brother Sonni worked with us, too, giving some of us voice lessons. But it's a mistake when people say Maurice taught us to dance, because he's got, like, two left feet. He can't dance at all.

Jonathan:

It was all Maurice's music. His system was to send us demo tapes first, so we could listen and learn the songs that way. Then, we'd rehearse and record them.

Jordan:

Maurice taught us a lot, we owe him a lot, but I tell you, it bugs me when people say that Maurice taught us to have soul. It wasn't anything like that. If you ask me, I always had soul. I think all of us have always been able to dance. And I always had rhythm. Maurice enlightened us on a lot of things. You know what's funny—I think I learned more from him than he actually taught me. I learned just by watching him. But he didn't wind us up like toys and make us what we are.

(© 1989 Larry Busacca)

Jonathan:

Mary helped mold us in the earliest stages, when it was real important. She never let us swear. She just really disciplined us. If she said, "Go home and practice your dance steps," you knew you'd better go home and practice your dance steps!

Donnie:

There's no one questioning that it was Maurice's vision. He had the big picture, he knew what we were going to be. But I don't see why people "dis" us [are disrespectful to us] because of that. Every music group was *someone's* idea. That doesn't make the other members of the group any less talented, or less important.

Danny:

Even more than Maurice, Mary guided us through the first years of us being together. Through his connections, Maurice got us the gigs, but Mary was the one who'd take us home from rehearsal each night, she was the one who took us to and from the shows. She had this old Mustang, and we'd crowd in. As we got taller, we had to scrunch down in the car, and we'd complain to her about how uncomfortable it was. But she'd be there every day at rehearsals, drilling us, "Get your mikes in your faces! Put your mikes up to your mouths!" In the beginning, she really took care of us.

TOP LEFT:
Dick Scott (© 1989 Todd Kaplan)

BOTTOM LEFT:
An early Kids look, 1986 (courtesy Marlene Putman)

RIGHT:
(courtesy Betty Wood)

Joe:

We all wore the same exact outfits, and Mary used to take pictures of us. I was so much smaller than the other guys—and my hair was totally straight. I don't know what happened—I reached puberty, and it curled up!

Jordan:

We rehearsed in different places. Sometimes it was in our basement, and other times it was at the Lee School, a community school nearby. We practiced the songs Maurice gave us, and we worked with a choreographer. I liked the songs, even though at the time I was listening to rap music and stuff. This was very different, but I still liked it. The songs were catchy, they were great. You couldn't help but love them. And the songs that we were practicing, right from the start in those early days, were the songs that ended up on our first album.

Donnie:

I liked most of the songs, I was really into it. After rehearsal, I'd go back home, shut the door to my room and practice some more.

WHAT'S A NYNUK?

Donnie:

Nynuk was the name of the group. It was something Maurice thought up, and no one really knows what it means or why he wanted to use it. But that was the name, before any of us even joined. It was pronounced "Na-nook," as in "Nanook of the North." And we all hated it.

Jordan:

When I got into the group, they told me the name, and I hated it. When I would tell people I was in a group, I wouldn't say the name. They would say, "Well, what's the name of your group?" And I would go, "It doesn't have a name yet," or, "We're still talking about a name."

Joe:

But we never asked Maurice to change it. We didn't really speak up for ourselves in the beginning.

Jordan:

That's true. Back in those days, I didn't speak up for anything. Maurice always decided who would do leads on each song. Mostly, it was Joe or Donnie. For the longest time I wanted to sing leads, and I didn't speak up. I wanted Maurice to let me sing a lead, or at least give me a chance, 'cause I knew I could do it. I knew I had it in me, and it was just a matter of time. But in the beginning, I didn't speak up for anything really.

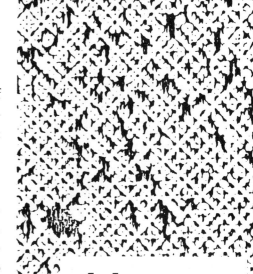

> **They had this idea that their group could be the new Osmond brothers or the Jackson 5 and they were looking for someone with a high voice to be the 'Donny Osmond' or the 'Michael Jackson.'**
>
> **—JOE**

Donnie:

The name didn't get changed until we went to sign up with Columbia Records and they said it had to be changed. So we took our name from a rap I wrote called "New Kids On The Block" that was on our first album. Everyone was real happy when our name was changed.

OUR FIRST SHOWS

Danny:

After a while, Maurice decided we were ready to do some showcases. Basically, we did talent shows and little shows at schools, benefits, anything to groom us and get us ready, give us experience.

Jordan:

I remember the first show we did, how I felt. I was petrified. I did have some lead parts by that time, but mostly I was in the background. When my lead parts came up, I wouldn't leave my mike stand, I wouldn't go out front and dance or do anything—I stayed in the back. I was so scared.

Joe:

Whenever we did a talent show or whatever, we'd come away with great ideas for new shows. So that's how we started getting ideas and having our own input into our shows.

ABOVE:
NYNUK, 1985 (courtesy Betty Wood)

RIGHT:
(© 1986 CBS Records, Inc. Courtesy Columbia Records)

OPPOSITE:
(© 1986 CBS Records, Inc. Courtesy Columbia Records)

Jonathan:

I'll never forget our first show. For a week before the show I could not eat, and I don't even know how I got through the show, because my knees were shaking so bad, it was crazy. I don't even know how I could stand, they were shaking so bad. I was just so nervous. This was at the Lee School in Boston. I remember, on the day of the show I had to force myself to eat a peanut butter and jelly sandwich.

Joe:

The first six months, we really only played in small clubs. It seemed like we were doing clubs forever. Sometimes only four or five people would show up. Then we started doing places that were a little bit bigger, and we started to get some applause. But I think it was the fun of just being onstage, with or without applause, that kept us alive.

Danny:

We had four years before we had any real success. I remember once we opened for the group Lisa Lisa at a club in Boston called Lansdowne 9, and the college radio station began talking about us.

Jonathan:

Our early audiences were mainly black, because that's where Maurice had his connections. They accepted us right away. I think they were astounded, but they enjoyed us.

Jordan:

All our audiences, even from the very beginning, have been pretty good, to tell you the truth. I think ever since the beginning, we've always been good onstage, and we've always had a lot of energy. Definitely, the stage is one of our strong points.

Of course, there were those days when I felt like just walkin' off the stage in the middle of a show because things would go wrong. I would do a spin, and the mike cords would wrap around my feet, and I would just be totally entwined in the microphone wires. I would do a move and kick the mike stand into the crowd, things like that.

But now, I could trip and fall onstage and not really care. It just wouldn't faze me, because if the audience sees you get up from a fall and recover, they'll cheer you all the more, really. They'll say, "Yea!"

EARLY TRAVELS

Jonathan:

When we first started traveling, we would just do shows in and around Boston. Then we started getting gigs in New York and New Jersey. So we'd rent a car and drive out.

" **Mary worked us really hard, from 5:30 to 9 PM every day after school, five days a week. It was *hard*. We'd come home beat tired and we'd have to go to school the next day.** "

—JORDAN

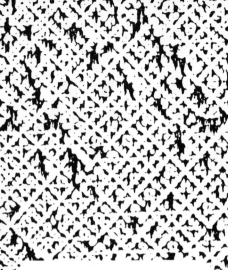

> **"** I'll never forget our first show. For a week before the show I could not eat, and I don't even know how I got through the show, because my knees were shaking so bad. **"**
>
> **—JONATHAN**

Then it got to the point where we had a mobile home. It had one bed in the back, and there were five of us and our road manager, Peter Work. All five of us Kids and Peter used to sleep in the back in that one bed. I always remember how funny it was when we used to hit the bumps on the highway, and we'd all go flying up and come down and land in a different position.

Danny:

As the years went on, we had a million tour buses. In the beginning, we'd always get the cheapest one, so it would always end up breaking down. We've gone through buses left and right, they were always breaking down.

Joe:

When we first went on tour, we stayed in hotels, but we didn't have our own rooms like we do now. It was usually Danny and me staying in one room, and Jordan, Donnie, and Jon in another. Every night we had fights. Every night, another one of us would be saying, "Man, I'm out of here!"

OUR FIRST BIG CONCERT TOUR

Jonathan:

We were out on the road before anyone had heard of *Hangin' Tough*. There was a time I can remember when we were doing a lot of county fairs, and they were just so crazy. We ended up in some dust-bowl places, in the craziest places. There was hay on the stage and chickens running around underneath the stage. I felt like, "What are we doing here?" But I think when we look back on all those times, it's like they were meant to be. It's just part of the growing process. At the time, we'd be thinking, "Why are we doing this?" But now, I can see why we did it. The truth is, it's a lot more fun to look back at those moments than when they were actually happening.

Jordan:

It was hard, but in some ways it was easier on our first tour than it is now. No one really knew us, so when we played in amusement parks, we could go on all the rides after the show. When we stayed in hotels, we could use the hotel pool. When we were in Florida, we could go to the beach. Now, we can't do much of anything.

OUR BIG BREAK

Jonathan:

We got our big break because of two people—our booking agent, Jerry Ade, and the singer Tiffany. Tiffany was real well-known, and we shared the same agent, Jerry. He set it up for us to audition for her, so we could be on the same bill as Tiffany in concert. We auditioned in her dressing room. It was crazy.

But she said okay, we could open for her at her concerts. It was mostly girls going to her concerts, and they were there to see her. So when we were on stage, they weren't really as crazy as they are now, 'cause they didn't really know who we were.

I'm convinced that if it weren't for Tiffany, it would have taken us a lot longer to make it. It was really a critical time for us, because our record was just starting to break and we really needed the exposure. Tiffany could have said no. She could have said she didn't want us, and then we'd still be struggling. So, yeah, I think she saved us. She's a real cool kid.

But I think God meant for that to be, because Tiffany was a young kid, going through pretty much the same thing we're going through now. I think we all just understood each other. I think that's why all five of us remained close friends with her.

After that tour with Tiffany, that's what did it for us. It was our big break, but we were ready!

ABOVE LEFT:
Rehearsing the Christmas show, Jordan singing lead (© 1989 Larry Busacca)

ABOVE RIGHT:
(© 1989 Todd Kaplan)

MUSICAL STUFF: CHAPTER SEVEN

MAKING OUR ALBUMS

The dream of everyone trying to make it in the music world is to get a record contract. Naturally, that was our goal, too. Maurice thought he could do that for us, so when we were ready, he booked time at a recording studio called Mission Control, out in Westford, Massachusetts, a forty-minute drive from Dorchester. Mary would gather us up in her little gray Mustang and we'd go to record.

OUR FIRST ALBUM

Basically, we started with only four songs, "Be My Girl," "Angel," and "Stop It Girl," and one that Donnie wrote, a rap called "New Kids On The Block." It was basically Donnie and Joe on the leads in those days, but we were all pretty comfortable with the songs, because those were the ones Maurice first taught us, and that was our "set" when we performed.

When Maurice was satisfied with the way those four tracks came out in the studio, he took the tape—it's called a demo tape—down to New York, where all the big record companies are. He played the tape for them, in hopes that we'd be picked up and signed right away. Well, it didn't happen right away. Most of the record companies said, "Well, we don't know, we're not sure," stuff like that. But Maurice didn't get frustrated; he just kept on trying.

Finally, in 1986, Columbia Records said they'd take a chance on us. Originally, we signed for only one 12″ single, with an album to follow if the single took off. But for some reason, it worked out that we got to do the whole first album. Since by that time, Columbia Records wanted our name changed, we took it from the name of Donnie's rap and used *New Kids On The Block* as the title of our first album, too.

Aside from the four songs we knew, that album also included another rap written by Donnie, "Are You Down?" Maurice pretty much decided which other songs were going to be on the album and figured out whose voice fit best for the leads on each one. We had "I Wanna Be Loved By You," which we all had parts on; "Popsicle," which was Joe's lead; "Don't Give Up On Me"; "Treat Me Right"; and, of course, "Didn't I Blow Your Mind?" Some of the songs were ones Maurice had written a long time ago, and others were fresh for us.

Maurice is a real creative genius, but he's not always predictable. One day we went to the studio all prepared to do one song, but when we got there, we found he'd changed his mind at the last minute. We recorded "Be My Girl" that day because he'd had a dream about it the night before. That's the way it is with Maurice.

We thought the album was great, but more than that, we were so excited to actually be signed to a big record label. Just to *have* an album, that was beyond our wildest dreams. But we were beginning to believe it now.

Maurice delivered the album to Columbia, and for a while we didn't hear anything about it. We didn't make any videos for it, we never even knew that the first single had been released. One day we were sitting in the dining room at Jonathan and Jordan's house. Mary had called a rehearsal, and we were meeting there. She took out her briefcase and said, "Wonder what's in here?" It was the vinyl 12″ of "Be My Girl," our first single—and we went ballistic. We couldn't believe it. We were so happy, we practically lost our minds. We ran into the living room and put it on the turntable and just watched it spin. We were transfixed, it had real grooves and everything—a real record! For all of us, that was one of our happiest moments ever. Donnie grabbed his copy and *ran* all the way home to show his family, he was so excited.

"Be My Girl" actually even made it onto the Top 100 singles chart. It came in at number 90 "with a bullet," which meant that at first, it looked like it was going to do real well. It didn't. The following week, it lost its bullet, and by the third week, it was off the charts altogether. But we weren't too bummed. Nothing could take away from the happiness we felt at having a real, concrete record with our name on it. We were more concerned that people we knew finally saw we had a record out. We were just glad to prove to people that we were for real.

That first time we saw it on the charts was almost as exciting. We were actually screaming when we saw it listed in *Billboard*, the music industry trade paper.

The next two singles that were released—"Stop It Girl" and "Didn't I?"—never made it to *Billboard*. "Didn't I?" *was* released 'way back then but went nowhere.

HANGIN' TOUGH

Our album, which we were so excited about, had kind of come and gone within six months, and our record company was frankly a little skeptical about giving us a second chance. But they decided to go for it, and so we did. Sure, we were disappointed that we didn't have a hit that first time around, but it only made us more determined to succeed with the next one. We were going to get back to rehearsals and back to the studio and come out with an incredible album. Our attitude was, we'd failed once, but we were going to hang tough and try again. And that's exactly where the name of the album came from!

Hangin' Tough was recorded both at Mission Control and at the studio in Maurice's home, House Of Hits. Since we'd spent so much time in the recording studio for *New Kids On The Block*, we'd learned a lot, and we actually had a hand in the producing and engineering of *Hangin' Tough*.

But at that time, Maurice didn't really have a great recording facility at his home—there really was no money. He had only one keyboard, and there was almost no soundproofing. So anytime a plane flew overhead, or even a car drove by, we'd have to stop recording, or those sounds would end up on our record! Just goes to show, you don't need to spend a fortune to put out a successful record.

Now we can look back and realize that it's a much better album musically than the first one, but in truth, we can't say we knew that then. We'd become real attached to *New Kids On The Block*, and in our minds, we weren't sure that this new one was any better. Jordan admits that when he first heard "Please Don't Go Girl" and even "I'll Be Lovin' You (Forever)," he didn't even like them. Those two ballads, which ended up being his favorite songs later on, just didn't grab him when

TOP:
Liberty Weekend (courtesy Marlene Putman)

MIDDLE:
December 1988: Joe, Maurice and Danny in Hawaii (courtesy Betty Wood)

BOTTOM:
Santa Claus—Jordan
(© 1988 Todd Kaplan)

he heard them in their earliest stages. And Jon admitted that when he first heard *Hangin' Tough* all mixed together, he thought it stunk! Donnie, on the other hand, always seemed to know this album was going to be huge, from the minute we finished recording it. Donnie could feel it; he knew it was going to happen.

Luckily, Donnie turned out to be right, for it's sold something like twelve million copies. But even *Hangin' Tough* took a long time getting onto the charts. It was actually released in 1988, but the first single, "Please Don't Go Girl," didn't start to break until that summer. That's why it was so important for us to get that concert gig with Tiffany at just that time. It made all the difference.

Our record company gave us a big push with *Hangin' Tough*, too. They put a big marketing effort behind it—we did a major stand at Disneyworld where they flew in high school kids to be in the audience—and we're grateful to them, too.

We did our first videos for *Hangin' Tough*. We did four altogether—"Please Don't Go Girl," "(You Got It) The Right Stuff," "I'll Be Lovin' You (Forever)," and "Hangin' Tough"—and we don't doubt that those videos helped get us airplay, too.

We've learned a lot, but probably the most important lesson is that it takes a humongous amount of people who believe in you and who are dedicated, to get your record out and take it to the point where audiences get to hear it. We thank each and every one of them!

STEP BY STEP

We got so busy going on tour for *Hangin' Tough* that the good, old days of spending months in the recording studio became a thing of the past real fast. We recorded our *Merry, Merry Christmas* album pretty much totally on the road! We never realized you could do that, but Maurice showed us how. He'd just join us on the road, and in any spare moments, we'd learn the new material, rehearse, and do the actual recording in our hotel rooms—often with fans right outside. Maurice would put mattresses up around the room so that there was no echo, and we'd just do our parts. When we wanted an echo, we'd go into the hotel bathrooms, because that's where we'd get it! Then Maurice would take the recordings back to the studio, where he'd do the mixing, putting in the instruments and all that. Pretty amazing!

That's pretty much the way it was with some of the tracks for *Step By Step*, our newest album. We're really proud of it and think it shows how we've progressed. Maurice wrote all the songs, but we helped out on some of the tracks with the writing and the engineering, too. The only thing we didn't get to do is play instruments on *Step By Step*, and that's just because there wasn't time.

Jordan does a lot of the leads on *Step By Step*. His favorite is "Let's Try It Again," because it reminds him of the old group the Stylistics, which he loves. He shares lead vocals with Danny on it. It's a slow song, and although Jordan loves the rockers, he feels he can put more feeling, more beauty into the ballads. He's also the lead voice on "Valentine Girl" and "Honey, Don'tcha Leave Me Tonight." The title track, "Step By Step," is also Jordan's lead: it's a great song with a fast groove that you just have to move to; and we love the Beatles-sounding track, "Tonight." There's a new reggae song on the album that Donnie does leads on; this time, Jonathan gets to step up front and center on "Happy Birthday"; and Joe sings lead on "Where Do I Go From Here?"

One song on *Step By Step* that we all wrote together is called "Games." It's our message to people who talk junk about us—it's aimed at the people who criticize us.

We plan on a bunch of videos right away, which is cool, because we love doing videos. It's almost as good as live performances.

Our summer tour is where we'll be singing the songs from *Step By Step* for the first time. It's called Magic Summer, and we hope to make it just that for all our fans.

> " We've learned a lot but probably the most important lesson is that it takes a humongous amount of people who believe in you and are dedicated, to get your record out and take it to the point where audiences get to hear it. We thank each and every one of them! "

Maurice Starr (© 1990 Lavalais Studios)

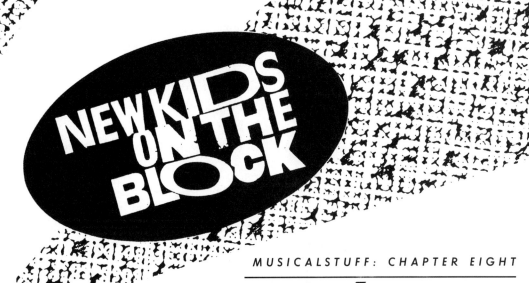

NEW KIDS ON THE BLOCK

VIPS (VERY IMPORTANT PEOPLE)

Aside from our families—and our fans, of course, who *really* put us on top—there are other people who've played a large role in our success. We're very lucky to have them in our corner, and we'd like to introduce them to you. This is our chance to say, "Thanks, guys!"

MAURICE STARR

Maurice is our producer, and it was his idea, back in Boston in 1984, to get us together. But in music circles, Maurice was a "Starr" before we ever came along. He's an extremely gifted and talented musician—seems like there's not an instrument he can't play. He's a singer, entertainer, songwriter, and producer. He discovered the pop group New Edition, which, at the time, was fronted by Bobby Brown, who went on to megasuccess with records like "My Prerogative."

Maurice auditioned each of us and gave us the chance. He taught us his music and shared with us the secrets of the "old school" of classic entertainers like James Brown and the Jackson 5. None of us had ever looked up to a musician before we met Maurice. Just by watching and listening to him, we absorbed so much. He had a way of talking and teaching—he's so jive—that kinda made you see it *his* way and kinda made you realize he was usually right.

But there's more to our relationship with Maurice than just teacher/ producer and students. We've come to know him as someone kind, someone who wouldn't hurt a fly, someone who is always there for us when we need him. He made us believe that we could really *be* something. New Kids On The Block was his vision. He always saw the big picture, even before there was much of anything to draw it with. He made us believe in ourselves. We love him.

MARY ALFORD

Mary doesn't get a lot of attention in the press, and that's an oversight. Partly it's because she doesn't work with us now, but she was instrumental in getting us started. Mary is a talent manager in Boston who just happens to live in Dorchester, so she spoke our language right from the start.

If Maurice saw the big picture, Mary filled in all the details. She was the one who started the search and found Donnie, and the one who ended the search by finding Joe. She was the one who came to our houses, picked us up, took us to rehearsals, and drove each of us back home at night.

Maurice was creating new music and finding places for us to perform; Mary was the hands-on person who actually rehearsed us and taught us discipline. She was the force we needed back then. She helped mold us. Mary was someone who helped push the snowball and got it rolling.

DICK SCOTT

Dick is our manager, and has been with us almost from the very beginning. He's big-time and has always managed Maurice Starr's career. Before that, he was a head honcho at CBS Records and worked with some of the biggest stars in the music business, including Diana Ross. So he really knows what he's doing.

If we had never met Dick, we wouldn't be where we are today. There's just no question about that. He's the main reason we've come this far. He's put so much of his time, his money, his *everything* into us. He always believed in us, right from the start. We owe him a lot.

TOP:
Mary Alford (© 1989 Larry Busacca)

BOTTOM:
Dick Scott (© 1989 Larry Busacca)

Dick Scott guides our career; he is the master builder of it all. He has final say on everything. He advises us about almost every facet of the business. He paints the big picture: he knows when and how we should move into the overseas market, do television, make movies, which deals we should sign, and which offers we should turn down. He never does anything just for the money. He has our best interests at heart, and we know that totally. He does everything for us. When Dick says, "I have your whole lives planned for you," we can be sure that he does and that it's gonna be totally cool. Straight up, he's the best manager in the world.

But Dick Scott is more than just a manager to us. He's like a father figure and our best friend, too. We go to him for advice on everything, not just career things, but personal problems, too. We look for his opinions on everything, and we can talk to him, as a group, or as individuals, about anything. He loves us and we love him very much.

PETER WORK

His middle name should be "Makes It" because Peter is the guy who "Makes It Work" when we're on tour. Peter is our tour manager—the man who travels with us, and is, in fact, our "Dick Scott on the road." He coordinates everything for us through Dick's office, plans our personal and professional schedules, and knows exactly where each of us is, twenty-four hours a day, seven days a week. When unexpected things come up—and they always do—Peter's the guy who gets it all taken care of, and in such a way that we don't miss a step. Peter makes sure everything gets done, that we do what we have to do, and that we do it right. He handles our press interviews and just about everything else on the road. And since we're on the road most of the year, Peter's the point person, the number-one man in charge of us. Without Peter, there is no "us" on the road; it's as simple as that.

Dick brought Peter on board when we went on the road for the first time. It was just us five Kids and Peter Work for a long time. So that is special.

Beyond all that, Peter's a friend. He's always there, no matter what. Yet he's so cool, so down, that sometimes we don't know how he gets the job done. But he does. Peter's real jive, he's always there for a laugh, and if you just need to chill with someone, he's the one. He's a good psychologist too. We couldn't "work" without him!

CATHY MCLAUGHLIN

Cathy is our assistant tour manager and advance person. She is just the best. She joined us on our last tour, and we don't know how we got

TOP:
Peter Work (© 1989 Todd Kaplan)

BOTTOM:
Cathy McLaughlin (© 1989 Larry Busacca)

along without her. Cathy left the Kennedy School of Government at Harvard to work with us. She also worked on the Dukakis presidential campaign—she *really* knows how to get things done, big-time.

Along with Peter, she handles all our press interviews on the road. She also arranges for and takes care of all the people we "Meet and Greet" backstage at our shows—she's the lady in charge of the backstage passes and complimentary tickets. She fields all requests. She has amazing energy and handles all the logistics of moving us from one place to another. She's like "information central," on top of everything at every moment. We're not really sure when she sleeps or eats.

Cathy also helps with our personal stuff on the road. She's too young to be called "our mother," but the truth is she does a lot of stuff that mothers do. When we want to fly our family or friends out to travel with us on tour, Cathy makes all the arrangements. She always gets things done 100 percent. We all know we can count on her, and that means a lot. We love you, Cathy!

BARRY ROSENTHAL, MARK WEINER, BOB WOOLF, & THE DUKE

They're not on the road with us, and they don't manage our careers or have anything to do with our music, but Barry Rosenthal (our lawyer), Mark Weiner (Dick and Maurice's lawyer), and Bob Woolf (along with John Dukakis), are key people in the New Kids family. Bob Woolf is our business manager and takes care of all of our finances, individually and as a group, making sure we don't get ripped off.

Before there *was* a New Kids On The Block, we'd heard of Bob Woolf. He's very famous, not only in Boston, but all over, because he's the big-time agent who handles the careers of all our sports heroes, like Larry Bird, Joe Montana, and Doug Flutie—all the guys we looked up to when we were growing up. It's so cool that now we're handled by the same team.

Barry, Mark, Bob, and John are great guys, great professionals, and they've been very hospitable to us and to our families. We trust them totally, and we think of them as our friends.

JERRY ADE

His is another name our fans might not be familiar with, but he's a pro who was with us before we hit it big, and without whom we might not have hit it so big. Jerry is our booking agent, which means he works closely with Dick Scott to determine what cities and arenas we're going to play and fills our bill with exciting opening acts.

In fact, it was Jerry who gave us our big shot at being an opening act, back in the summer of 1988. He's Tiffany's agent, and it was his idea to get us on the concert bill with her; he set up our audition and set the wheels in motion. Jerry knew it was an important time for us, and giving us just the right exposure—to Tiffany's teen audience—was what turned the tide for us.

We're proud to say Jerry's still our booking agent today, and we hope he always will be.

OUR PERSONAL SECURITY: BIZCUT, ROBO, BUTCH, & AL

These guys are our bodyguards—but they're also our best friends. They're with us *all* the time, even more than Peter or Cathy. We may go places without each other, but we're never without one of our bodyguards. It's not so much that we need them to "protect" us from our fans; they're there to make sure nobody gets hurt when we *do* go out in public. Our bodyguards are the nicest people. They're so great with our fans, they have their *own* fans! See, with us, it's a family thing. We've never thought of our bodyguards as people who work for us. It's more like they're our friends, and they have special places in our hearts.

Steve "Bizcut" Walker has been with us since 1987. He travels on the tour bus with Donnie, Danny, and Joe. We always seem to be watching movies on the bus with Bizcut, even though he usually falls asleep about one minute into the movie!

Clyde "Butch" Perry is the guy who taught Danny all about fitness. He's a body builder and usually goes to the gym with Danny. He's also on the Donnie/Danny/Joe bus. He's the kind of guy we can just be boys with, pounding on him, wrestling around with him. He's like our brother.

Steve "Robo" Chandler travels with the Knight brothers, and he's very street, very smart, and a good talker. He's chillin', he's down, and we love him.

Same with Al Grissinger. He's always right on the spot for whatever you want—a burger at three A.M. or help with your trunk. Al always agrees with us, he's funny, but a man of few words.

AND ALL THE OTHERS

There are so many other people who help us that it would take a whole book all by itself to mention all of them. But without each and every one, our records wouldn't get out, our videos wouldn't get made, *we* wouldn't be able to come to your town and put on a show. The guys who set up and take down our stage for every single show; the soundmen; the lighting guys; the engineers; the wardrobe, hair, and makeup guys; the pyrotechnics and laser experts who create the special effects, the video crew; our band; our announcer; and all the roadies—each one does a job that's just as important as ours. We think of them as family, and we wish all of them could stand up and take a bow.

OPPOSITE PAGE, TOP TO BOTTOM:
Barry Rosenthal (© 1989 Larry Busacca)

Mark Weiner (© 1989 Larry Busacca)

Bob Woolf (© 1989 Larry Busacca)

John Dukakis (photo by Leslie Miller)

THIS PAGE, TOP TO BOTTOM:
Jerry Ade (© 1989 Larry Busacca)

With Butch (© 1989 Larry Busacca)

With Bizcut (© 1989 Larry Busacca)

Zonked! (courtesy Marlene Putman)

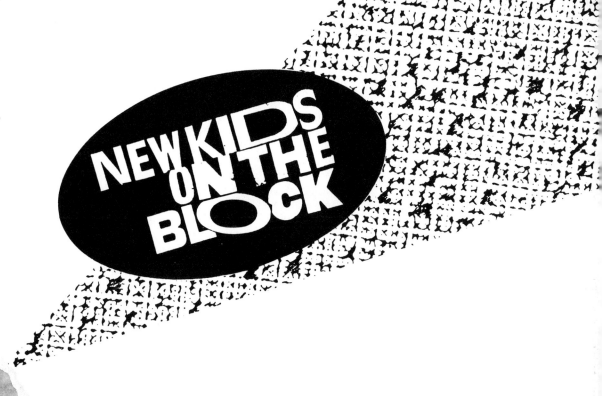

MUSICALSTUFF: CHAPTER NINE

ON THE ROAD

We spend a lot of time on the road, doing concerts all over the country. We go out so we can bring our show to all the fans who want to see us, and we're really happy to do that. It's great, but it's weird, 'cause we can be in a different city every single night—and sometimes, we nearly lose track of where we are. Most people don't understand what life on the road is really like, so we'd like to take this chapter to share it with you.

THE TOUR BUSES

Our fans know that we travel from concert to concert in big buses. Sometimes, right after a show, we'll board the buses and travel all night to the next city. Other times, we'll sleep in a hotel and get on the bus the next day. Whether we travel at night or during the day depends on how far it is to the next gig.

When we started out, we only had one bus, but for our last tour we had seven. Most of them are for our band, our crew, and our stuff. Only two of them are for us Kids. There are two buses that have Indian scenes painted on the side of them, and a lot of people think those are the ones we're on, but they're not. Our crew uses those buses. We've got two of the newer ones, but that will probably change for our summer tour.

We had our buses specially built for us. In the front of each bus is a little kitchen area, with a mini-fridge (that's always stocked with fruit and snacks and soft drinks), a microwave, and a coffee machine, though no one really drinks coffee, so we hardly ever use that. There's a table and two bench seats on one side and a couch on the other. We've got one TV and a VCR in this part of the bus, too.

Toward the back—actually in the middle of the bus—is where our bunks are. Usually buses that groups use have twelve bunks, but ours have only six. They're stacked up three bunks high, and each one has a curtain so it can be totally dark and we can actually get some sleep. We used to have these skinny mattresses, but now we have regular-size ones, so we can be more comfortable. That's important, because we spend anywhere from four to twelve hours a day on the bus! Donnie is the only one who doesn't really care about the size of the mattresses— he sleeps on the floor. But that's just Donnie! In our bunk area there's also a small bathroom, kind of like the ones you find on an airplane, and we have these humongous closets there, too.

In the back of the bus, after the bunks, is another sitting area. It's got a table and couches all around, and built in along the walls are stereos, more VCRs, and another TV.

We asked for our buses to be cheery and well lit, because usually tour buses are so dark. So we got fluorescent lights going all the way down the hallway. And we got nice etched-glass mirrors.

We divided up who goes on which bus by what we like to do. Since Donnie, Danny, and Joe like to play Nintendo, they're on one bus together. Two of our bodyguards, Butch and Bizcut, are also on that bus, so it's kind of crowded. The other bus is for Jordan and Jonathan, Robo the bodyguard, and our road manager, Peter Work.

What usually happens on the bus is that Danny and Bizcut will take over the front, settle in on the couch, and switch on a movie; we've got tons of cassettes. Donnie and Joe usually start out in the back with their Nintendo set.

Jordan and Jonathan watch a lot of concert videos. Lately it's been Madonna and Janet Jackson. Jordan watches Michael Jackson in concert over and over again! Jonathan's the one who likes to keep the bus neat. He's always cleaning it up.

Another thing we do on the buses that we don't get a chance to do in

> **Another thing we do on the buses that we don't get a chance to do in other places on the road is just talk, and that's important for us. And, of course, we sleep—big-time. Especially Jonathan and Jordan. They sleep the most.**

other places on the road is just talk, and that's important for us. And, of course, we sleep—big-time. Especially Jonathan and Jordan. They sleep the most.

A lot of people have asked us why we don't save time and fly from concert to concert, but we really like our buses. It's like if we go on an airplane, it's just another plane. We're in a different hotel room every night. The bus is really the only stable environment that we have. It's home.

OUR TOY TRUCK

Aside from the tour buses that we travel on, we also have a truck that follows along on the road with us. We call it our toy truck, and we just got it for our last tour. In some towns we go to it's really hard for us to get out and do things, because we're recognized everywhere we go. So we got the idea to bring things with us. That gives us a way to let off some steam, and to just play.

In our toy truck we have motorized scooters, mopeds, gopeds, hockey masks and equipment, roller skates, and all kinds of other stuff. Every single day we're out in the parking lot of the hotel we're staying in, riding around on our scooters, or even taking out a moped and going around town, to a restaurant or something. Sometimes, if

November 29, 1989—Matthew bringing Jonathan a birthday cake on stage! (© 1989 Larry Busacca)

the venue isn't too far from the hotel, we'll even ride our mopeds to the concert. The mopeds drive our manager Dick Scott crazy. He's afraid that we'll get hurt. We've really been havin' fun with them.

WHAT WE DO ON THE ROAD

Even though we spend a lot of time just getting from place to place, there are usually a few hours in each day to do something for fun. Danny never has a problem deciding what he's going to do: he and our bodyguard Butch go to the nearest gym in every town and work out. He goes six days a week, or tries to, anyway. It's real important to him, not just to look good, but for his mental state as well. And it's Danny who tries to eat right on the road—no junk food, just lots of fruit and good stuff.

The rest of us like to check out the shopping in any new town we visit. So usually, after we get to a hotel, we'll ask where the nearest cool mall is. We never go all five of us—that would be crazy—but one or two of us with a security person usually works out okay. We've got some collection of stuff from our on-the-road shopping sprees!

AT THE HOTEL

In most cities, we'll be spending some time at a hotel. In the big cities, it's hard for the fans to find us; but in the smaller places, they usually figure out where we're staying. That's cool. It's kinda nice to be "welcomed" to any new place. We try to give autographs when there's time and when we can, but sometimes we're honestly just too rushed or tired.

Usually, we're all on the same floor of the hotels we stay at, but it wouldn't be too easy to try and call us—we're all registered under code names, which change from tour to tour. We don't mess up hotels like some other bands we've heard about. Basically, the worst we'll do is have a water fight or something. We order a lot of room service (pizza's big on our list), and we watch whatever movies are on the cable TV. Since there's never time to go to a new movie that's out in the theaters, we catch up a lot, between the VCRs on the bus and the TV in the hotels.

IT'S GREAT, BUT . . .

We gotta be honest, 'cause this is our book, right? And we want our fans to know how we really feel. Along with all the fun, there are some frustrating things about being on the road. We miss our homes and our families, and that can be a bummer. We miss the everyday routines. Some of us—mainly Jonathan—worry about how things are coming along at home, if things are getting done all right, and how our moms are doing. When you think about it, being on the road—living out of a suitcase, never sitting down to a home-cooked meal or doing our laundry (okay, Jonathan *does* do his own laundry on the road), not hanging with our friends—it's a weird way to live for such a long time.

Sometimes, if we're in one place for more than a day, we do get to fly our family and friends out to spend time with us. That helps a lot. Some of our friends come on the bus with us, and that way they can understand what we actually do on the road. It makes us feel good when we can let our people experience some of this stuff.

The other thing is that no matter how many places we go—and we've been to all fifty states, and Europe and Japan, too—we hardly ever get to see any of the famous sights. It's just kind of aggravating. The way we see it, most kids don't even get to leave their own neighborhoods, and here we have the chance to travel all over the world, and we've hardly seen anything. When we were in Memphis, we really wanted to see Graceland, but there was no time. About the only famous place we did get to spend time at is Disneyworld in Florida. We really loved that!

You can see that there are definitely ups and downs to being on the road, but when we get out there onstage, performing for 15,000 screaming, happy fans, we know one thing: it's all worth it!

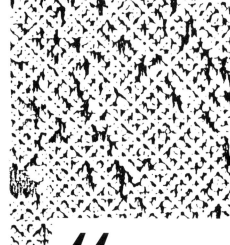

> " There are usually a few hours in each day to do something for fun. So after we get to a hotel, we'll ask where the nearest cool mall is. We never all go—all five of us—but one or two of us with a security person usually works out okay. "

Touching the ones we love (© 1989
Todd Kaplan)

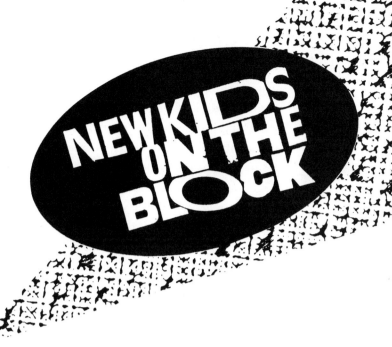

NEW KIDS ON THE BLOCK

IN CONCERT!

We love performing live, we love bringing our music to our fans—that's one thing we all agree on. We have 100 percent input into the shows. Our show is *our* show. We pretty much do everything. We do a lot of the choreography ourselves, and it was our idea to use the lasers and pyro—that is, the smoke, flames, and loud "explosions" you see and hear in the show. We don't always have a lot of time to prepare for a concert tour—last year, we only had eleven days!—but that's one of the reasons our shows are so spontaneous. Even *we* don't always know what we're going to do when we get up there!

It's as exciting for us as it is for every single person in the audience. We can't take you backstage with us, or up onstage with us, but we can tell you exactly what it's like: welcome to the world of New Kids In Concert!

A BACKSTAGE PASS

Not every place is the same, but usually we get to the venue—that's the arena, or stadium or whatever, where we're playing—earlier than you probably think. If we're scheduled to go on at 8:30 or something, we're usually backstage by 5:00 or so. If we don't come straight off our buses, we usually get there by limo (we have three limousines that travel with us), or we might take our mopeds to the venue.

We rehearse a little, but we don't do sound checks; our band and our sound people do that. They set up early so they can hear what kinds of echoes are bouncing off the walls.

It's usually set up backstage so there are dressing rooms for us, our band, our crew, and each of our opening acts. We usually get pretty friendly with our opening acts, and, of course, our band and crew are like family; so you can always find us in and out of everyone's dressing room, hanging out.

Backstage is where we usually eat dinner. There's a caterer who's hired to cook for all seventy of us, and even though we have our food in our dressing room, one or two of us can almost always be found on line with the crew. The food in our dressing room, in fact, sometimes ends up as the ammunition in a good food fight, one of the ways we've been known to let off steam before a concert. We also drink this energy drink, with natural herbs and stuff. We have a blender, and sometimes we mix bananas and ice cream and all this crazy carbohydrate powder. We don't even know what's in it half the time. It tastes nasty, but it works. It keeps up your energy.

At every show, we have something called Meet & Greet. That's where we get to meet some of the fans who are coming to the show that night. Usually, they're radio station contest winners, or fans who did something special and got a backstage pass. It's nice for us, because we don't always get to meet as many fans as we'd like to, and Meet & Greet is one small way of saying thanks, one-on-one.

But aside from people with official backstage passes, there are really not a whole lot of other "friends of friends of friends" backstage. Our backstage is relatively quiet and calm compared to others. It's not just that we need a little space before we go on, but this is our job—it's like going to the office, in a way—and we need to concentrate on doing the best job possible for our fans in the audience. That's who we're thinking about.

When our opening acts go on, that's when we get busy. Or that's when we should *start* to get busy, anyway. But we don't always. Sometimes, we'll still be poring over magazines that end up backstage, or digging through the gifts that fans send. Jordan sometimes sticks his head between the curtain in the back so he can watch the opening acts.

In our dressing room is where Uncle Rob (Robert Coleman)—that's what we call our wardrobe manager—has all our clothes set up, and we pick what we're going to start out in. We go through a few costume changes during the show, and Uncle Rob takes care of all that. With his help, we've got it down to a science—while two or three of us are onstage, the others are backstage, getting changed. We get our hair washed, combed, moussed, and sprayed, and our makeup put on by Brad Bowman—and we get psyched. Are we nervous? Sure, there are butterflies, but it's not really nervousness—it's more like anticipation and excitement. The truth is that we don't have much time to get nervous—we always wait till the last minute to get dressed, and then, it's like rush-rush-rush-rush-rush!

ONSTAGE!

Suddenly, or it seems like suddenly, we hear our announcer, Johnny Wright, talking about us to the audience. Johnny is great; he's been with us for years. Our cue is when he takes each microphone and tells the audience which of us stands where. Then...the audience hears, "Are you ready for Donnie, Jordan, Jonathan, Danny, and Joe, the five hardest-working kids in show biz—the New Kids On The Block!!"

Everyone is screaming—you can hear the screams backstage. And then the music gets real loud, the lights start flashing, and we fly up on stage—and its *total* pandemonium. It's the greatest rush, the greatest high—we love the screams, and the energy from the audience is intoxicating. We never wear earplugs; we like it loud!

Our audiences are crazy! They're crazy every night, and you can't beat it. You can't beat our crowd. A lot of people wonder whether we see the girls in the audience. Take it from us, we definitely do. A lot of people think because the lights are shining in our eyes, we can't really see, but the lights are always changing. We can't honestly see all the way to the back, but we can see at least half the arena. We can see the people on the sides, and if there are fans in the seats behind us, we turn around and can see them pretty clearly, too.

Each audience is a little different, and we try to play each one a little differently. If for some reason they're responding to what we're doing, but not that great, we try to give out 110 percent. We don't slack up. Instead, we give *them* more energy and hope they give it back. We feel that *we* are the entertainers, that it's our job to entertain and make that audience go crazy.

Of course, most audiences don't need our encouragement to go crazy. In the old days, before our security was real tight, kids used to sneak up on the stage and dance with us, and that was cool. One night,

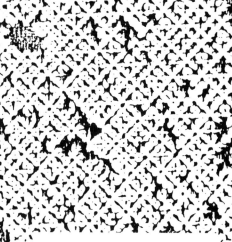

" We love all our songs, but the most meaningful is 'This One's For the Children...' Sometimes that song can really move us—and if you look real closely, there are times when one of us has gotten real teary while we're singing it. **"**

more recently, a girl got past our security, got up onstage, and came to "attack" us. Instinctively, like we all thought of this together, *we* all ran up and hugged her! It was great. Instead of her jumping on us, we jumped on her. That was a good one—boy, was she surprised!

Jordan's been "strangled" on stage by overzealous fans. He bent over into the audience, and two girls grabbed his hair and one grabbed the chain on his neck and pulled it—but he liked it; he thought it was fun.

Of course, there is one girl that we invite to come up on the stage, and that's the one Donnie will sing "Cover Girl" to. Because we're running around up there, we don't actually pick the girl who comes up. One of our bodyguards does that. He goes out looking for a little kid; we always take a little one. There's no real reason for doing that, just that we did it that way once and we kinda liked it. It was sweet. And besides, Donnie's afraid that if we bring up an older, hipper fan, she might start dancing real good and make *him* look real bad! Only kidding, Cheeze. (That's Donnie's nickname.)

At almost every show, fans throw things onto the stage. We know that they just want to make contact with us, see us pick it up, and it's usually cool, but sometimes they don't realize someone could get hurt. Some kids throw money, for some reason—coins. One of these days, one of us is going to step on one and go flying and end up with a broken leg. We also can't understand why some people throw lipstick, or chewed gum. That's weird. Flowers are nice, they're pretty and sentimental, but if we accidentally step on a bouquet of flowers, we could easily slide and fall.

All the gifts that people either toss up onstage or send backstage we have the ushers gather up. We really can't keep all the stuff. If we kept everything, we'd have ten warehouses full of stuff! So we accept it and look through all of it and take the names down and send thank you letters and stuff. We really *do* appreciate it, and we really do understand that it's all given to us out of love.

What we do is try to turn around and do something nice with the gifts. We send the teddy bears over to children's hospitals, and lots of times, the flowers will go to nursing homes. It's like love that's coming through us, and it's all doing good.

WHAT MAKES A GREAT SHOW

Of course, we *try* to give the best show every single night, but each of us has different things that make it great for him.

Jordan:

A great show for me is when I have total control, I feel totally confident—when I let loose. I know it's been a good show when I feel I

TOP:
Jonathan, Joe, and Jordan in the limo (courtesy Marlene Putman)

BOTTOM:
Joe getting ready for the show with Brad Bowman, who does our stage makeup (© 1989 Larry Busacca)

can do anything, when nothing holds me back from anything, when I'm not self-conscious at all; that's the best show. But I'm very critical of my performance. It's just that I click so good in some shows that I hold those up as a measuring stick.

I love the applause. A lot of people strive to be good because of the reception they get. They might not want to admit it, but that's an unconscious thing in everybody. They do it because the audience accepts it and appreciates it. I think that's the main thing.

Donnie:

I have a good show when I have good interaction with the fans. When I'm just loose and confident onstage, that's when I interact with them, and that's when I really make personal contact with five hundred people a night. Don't ever think I can't see you, or I'm not looking at you, because really, that's what I'm *trying* to do up there. That's all I'm thinking about up there. That can be good or bad, because if I'm in a really self-conscious mood, a certain person in the crowd can just catch my attention, and I'll be thinking about that person the whole show. I'll be really distracted.

But it can be good, because that's what I thrive on, the fans. Some nights it's so beautiful, because I feel so close to the fans, I feel like I can just do anything I want up onstage. That's when I really enjoy myself.

I wouldn't feel satisfied if I just went up there and ran around and

(© 1989 Todd Kaplan)

didn't interact with the audience. For me, that's my whole thing, that's what it's all about.

If for some reason the audience isn't too crazy, I try real hard to pick it up at the end of the show. In our last tour, I had the last two leads, "Cover Girl," and "Hangin' Tough." That's where I really want to pick up the pace; those songs have to be big. That's when I usually try to put *everything* into it; the last of my energy comes out there. Some nights I don't even realize how intense I get. I once split my leg open—I needed stitches—and didn't even know it.

Jonathan:

For me, it's different. I do see the girls in the audience, and they mean so much to me, but I feel weird. I feel like they might be thinking, "Why is he looking at me?" But then that's just me, 'cause I'm still just Jonathan Knight, and I guess I'm still a little insecure about that stuff. If I smile at someone and she doesn't smile back, I feel stupid.

Danny:

I love all our shows, but what makes it the best for me is when I see that someone in the audience is holding up a sign that says "I Love Danny." I appreciate that so much, because I'm, like, in the background; I'm not out front. So if someone has an "I Love Danny" sign, I'll look at them the whole show. I'll acknowledge them the whole show. Because it's something I will never take for granted, because a girl took the time out and did a sign. I love it, and I love when someone does that. In fact, that's the first thing I look for, as soon as I get onstage, I'll look around to see if anyone has a sign. I love the shows, but when someone has a sign, it's icing on the cake, my whole show is perfect.

Joe:

When we get the craziest onstage is when I'm havin' the most fun. Some nights, just spontaneously, we get nuts, wrestling and play-fighting and running up and down the ramps and stuff. And we all try and touch as many hands from the audience as we can. For me, the wilder the better.

OUR FAVORITE SONG

We love all our songs that we do in concert, but the most meaningful, for us, is "This One's For The Children." There's a message in that song, and sometimes we'll wonder if the fans are getting it, because they're screaming so loud. But we know in our hearts that they do. Sometimes that song can really move us—and if you look real closely, there are times when one of us has gotten real teary while we're singing it.

ENCORE!

We'll always come out for an encore. If we could, we'd stay on stage until no one wanted to see us anymore—we love it that much. After our encore—last tour it was "Hangin' Tough"—we don't run off the stage like most other groups do. We stay on as long as we can, sometimes just goofing around, being our crazy selves. But really, what we're doing up there is trying to thank each and every person in the audience, for all their love and support. We'll never take that for granted. For us, a great show is the greatest reward there is.

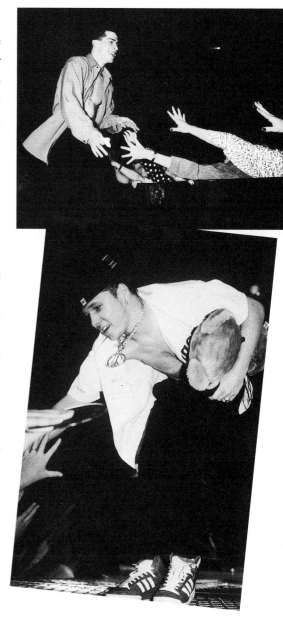

AND AWAY WE GO!

Most of the time, because of the security problems, we jump into the limos that are waiting to take us back to the hotel, or onto our buses. We don't even change into regular clothes, just get out of our sweaty stage outfits and throw on our terry cloth robes and hop into the limo. It looks like we're making a fast getaway, but pretty much we have to do it that way, or a riot might start.

But we don't always leave the venue right after the show is over. There are often interviews to do with the press, and that's okay with us. We'd rather talk to people after a show, because we're so hyped up, so keyed up that we couldn't go to sleep anyway. We've given some of our best interviews after midnight!

If there's one of us most likely to be staying at the venue after a show, it's Jonathan Knight. He sometimes likes to hang around and actually help the crew disassemble our huge stage. He helps with the cables and bringing down the speakers and stuff. He's done it so often, the road crew teases him that he's gonna get fired from New Kids and have to join the road crew.

WHEN THE SHOW IS OVER...

After we go back to our hotel, we hardly ever go to sleep. Joe's the only one who might even try. But we're so "up" that it takes hours and hours to unwind. We've become night people. We don't do major partying or anything, but we like to hang out with our bodyguards, in their rooms, order pizza or room service, watch movies and sports on TV. Or sometimes we just talk. We'll talk about the show we just did, compare how we think it went, and come up with great ideas for the next show. By the time we're done and ready to go to sleep, the next show isn't very far away!

TOP:
Feeling the heat! (© 1989 Todd Kaplan)

BOTTOM:
Donnie reaching out (© 1989 Larry Busacca)

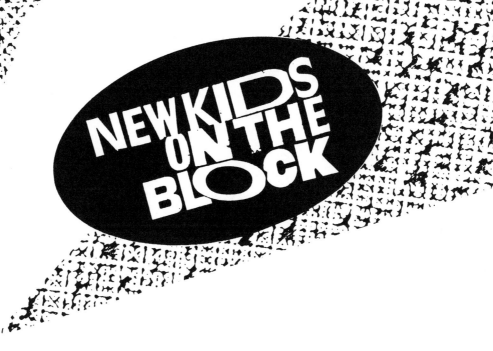

NEW KIDS ON THE BLOCK

REFLECTIONS ON...

*T*here are so many things we think about, so much to share with you; here are our individual and honest feelings about some things that mean a lot to us, or that just plain bug us, or that our fans are always asking about.

OUR FANS

Joe:

Our fans are the best fans any group could have. Our fans are what got us here, and they made us what we are today. As long as we keep them happy, that means we are successful. It doesn't matter what awards we win, as long as our fans are happy. They keep giving us their support and their love, and we keep giving them our music and performances and everything else. That's all that matters.

Jordan:

I really love 'em. Our fans stick up for us a lot, no matter what. I mean, if a radio station talks bad about us, a thousand fans will picket the radio station. Our fans are so loyal, and it's so great to see that. That's what I really love them for.

Jonathan:

Our fans put us up on the hill, and I love 'em for that. I love giving autographs, I love taking pictures with fans. But there's a time and a place for everything. I know most fans understand that two in the morning is not a great time to come knocking at my door—and some people do that.

I like it when I go somewhere and there are a few kids, not a whole crowd. If I'm driving in Boston and I see a few kids wearing NKOTB T-shirts, I'll just pull over, even if they don't see me. And I'll roll down the window and say hi and stuff like that.

Donnie:

Our fans are intelligent. They always retaliate against negative press. I'm so proud of our fans for doing that. Not because they're sticking up for us, but because so many people are misled by the press. But our fans will read something and know instinctively if it's true. They won't let themselves be misled. They seem to know what we're about, and they say things that amaze me.

It's nice to know—it's flattering to know—that we can make someone's whole day with just a smile, or an autograph or a hug. It's important for me to touch people. If they're reaching out and just want to be touched, it's not hard to do that.

I hate to leave fans who are waiting for an autograph. I know there are always going to be people who think we're not nice, some fans who are waiting to meet us, but we couldn't stop and talk or something like that. I hate to walk through a hotel lobby or some place and not be able to sign anything for them. If the bodyguard says, no, I try and say, "I'm sorry, I can't," just so they'll know that *I* know they're there but I just can't stop at that moment.

See, for me, that's what my success is, my relationship with the fans. When I'm doing good with them, onstage and off, that's when I feel good. That's when I'm a success in my own mind.

TOP:
Talking to the fans (© 1989 Larry Busacca)

BOTTOM:
Here we are with Arsenio Hall and Dick Scott (© 1989 Larry Busacca)

Danny:

Our fans are they hypest, the hypest kids in the 1990s! (Translation: They're the best!)

BEING FAMOUS

Danny:

I don't feel famous. I don't feel we are in the Hollywood limelight. You don't see us at the Hollywood parties. We aren't caught up in that. We're caught up more in the fun things, y'know, like performing, riding our scooters, and having fun. We don't go around saying phony things like, "We're large....Peace....Into the limo."

But I guess we are famous; that is, people know who we are. That's a nice feeling, but sometimes it puts you in a bind. Like this one time, I was at the gym, lifting some heavy weights. I was right in the middle of it, and this lady comes out of nowhere and asks for an autograph. Now what am I supposed to do? Drop the weights? I just said, as politely as I could, "Would you wait until I'm done with my workout?"

But I'm not complaining. I'm happy, and I have a great life—the best life.

Joe:

We live large. That's our way of saying we have things we never thought we would. None of us comes from wealthy homes; we're all working kids. We had our dreams like everyone else, but we never really thought they'd come true. Who could have imagined, growing up in a house with nine kids, that one day I'd be in national magazines, meeting famous people, riding in a limo, getting awards, having fans who know who we are and who love us? To us, that's livin' large.

But there's a price to pay for livin' large. It might be a small price, but you still pay it. Sometimes you want to be left alone. You can never depend on being left alone. Sometimes people won't mess with you, but you can never depend on it. So you really can't be alone.

Most of our fans are respectful, but there are some that get carried away at inappropriate times. I went to church Christmas Eve with my family, and people were taking pictures of me at church. People had video cameras. Not only was it disrespectful to me and my family, it was disrespectful to the church. I did not smile or sign autographs or do anything to encourage it.

Donnie:

I never mind signing autographs. Sometimes doing it, making contact with the fans, really helps me. I've never told this to anyone, but my grandmother died when we were in the middle of our tour. I was at her side in Boston when it happened, and then I flew back to Georgia to rejoin the group. I did the show that night, and afterward, I went back

> " There are some great things about being famous, and it's heart-warming to know that our fans love our work. I can't think of anything better. To get to express myself creatively, doing something I love, and end up being famous for it, this is beyond my wildest dreams. "
>
> —JORDAN

to the hotel. There were fans in the parking lot. I spent half the night in that parking lot, signing autographs. And the fans who did not run up and attack me, I went over to *them* and kinda said, "Thanks for not attacking me." But I did it as much for myself as for them. That night I needed *them*. I needed the connection, I needed their love. And I got it.

Then there's the other side of it. My whole family was in the hospital, in my grandmother's room. She was dying. We were all sitting around, crying, saying good-bye to her. It was a very private and painful moment. Suddenly this nurse comes in and asks me for my autograph. She makes this big scene, "It *is* you, it *is* you!" I think she should have had more sense at a moment like that.

Jonathan:

For me, being famous is the weirdest. 'Cause I was never one to get into all the craziness and make a big fuss. To me, I'm just *me*, so I can't figure out what the big deal is, why everybody is going so crazy. If I'm in the mall, people really think that's strange. I can understand how they feel, 'cause it's like they're used to seeing someone in a magazine and then all of a sudden this person walks past them in 3-D. They're gonna feel, "Oh, my God! What are you doing here?" Well, what I'm doing there is the same thing they're doing: shopping!

I think it's hard for fans to put themselves in our shoes. But if I'm in a store and suddenly there's a big crowd outside the window, looking in at me, I start to feel like a monkey in a zoo. I guess I've never been real comfortable in the spotlight. And it's a twenty-four-hour-a-day thing; you can't turn it off.

The other surprising thing I found out about being famous is that there's a lot of work involved! Much more than I ever imagined. When you see famous people, you think of limousines and airplanes and fur coats—even I had that perception. You think that it's a big, glamorous thing, everything is carefree. But after going through it, all the hard work, the sleeping on the bus, and the nights where you get only three hours' sleep, I can see that it's not so glamorous or carefree.

Jordan:

There are some great things about being famous, and it's heartwarming to know that our fans love our work. I can't think of anything better. To get to express myself creatively, doing something I love, and end up being famous for it—this is beyond my wildest dreams.

The only bad part is when some people think that we're totally public property. When you say, "No, I'm not totally public property," they get offended and call you a snob. The last thing I want to do is offend anyone, and I don't think I'm a snob, but here's an example of when I got in a real bind. Some girl, the other day, came up to me and said,

"Jordan, you should forgive your father; you really should." I don't know what she read or where she read it, but that stuff is really nobody's business but mine. It's just private. She doesn't know anything that's gone on between me and my father, and she doesn't know my feelings about it, because I've chosen not to make them public. That should be my right. I do owe our fans the best records and performances I'm capable of, and I'll always be grateful to them for everything, but there's a point where some go really overboard. That was one of them.

HAVE WE CHANGED?

Joe:

People ask us if being famous has changed us in any way, and speaking for myself, I would say no. I'm so deeply rooted in my values, I'm so family-oriented that I couldn't change even if I tried. I really treasure my values.

Jonathan:

I have changed, but only for the better. I used to be really insecure, and now I've become more confident. I can deal with people better than I used to. But as a person, I'm definitely the same. So many people who knew me a long time ago have said, "I can't believe you haven't changed at all." None of us has really changed, and I think that's what's so good about this group. People relate to us as the average boys next door. We are sincere, and they can see that.

Jordan:

I think by now I would see a change, and the only one I see is for the better. Same with the other guys. I haven't seen any egos. The only thing that I have to fight against is becoming too dependent on other people. A lot of stuff is done for us. I *do* worry about that sometimes. Because right now I wouldn't know how to fill out an income tax form or apply for my driver's license or credit card. I wouldn't know the first thing about buying a house, or buying a car—all of these things have been done for me. That worries me. I sometimes think if I have to face the real world, it's gonna be very hard for me. But I'm not worried about the inner me changing. My values will never change.

THE PRESS...& THOSE RUMORS!

Jonathan:

Anyone with a record out needs the press. They write about you and help spread the word. In the beginning, when you're trying to become

> " It doesn't matter what awards we win, as long as our fans are happy. They keep giving us their support and their love, and we keep giving them our music and performances. That's all that matters. "
>
> —JOE

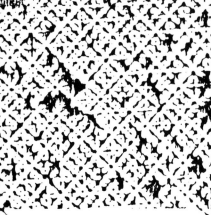

> **We're each other's best friends, but we're together so much that it's good to get away and be with other friends. I've made a lot of new friends on the road.**
>
> **—JONATHAN**

known, that's really important. Most of the time we've been treated fairly, and a lot of stuff is generally true. But sometimes the truth gets stretched out of proportion, and other times, they have nothing to write, so they write stuff that isn't true.

We want our fans to know that 99.9 percent of the rumors you hear about us are not true. No one's quitting. No one's married. We haven't been beat up by anyone, and we weren't in any airplane crashes. Joe did not have a heart attack, and Donnie was not caught smoking. It's like there's a new rumor every week. So if you hear a stupid rumor, you shouldn't have to think twice about whether it's true or not. Just use your common sense—of *course* they're not true.

Donnie:

It seems to take a lot for some of the press to write something good about us. We've been naive. Lots of times we've opened our hearts to interviewers, and we thought everything was going so well. Then it's a shock when they write all this negative stuff about us. They seem upset that young girls like us; they're annoyed at the screaming fans. They get so mad! Why are they so bothered by it? They're upset that we have the 900-number phone lines. They don't look at the positive side at all. They don't print—although we told them—that when we were first offered the 900 line, we turned it down, because it seemed to us like a get-rich-quick thing, and we didn't want to do that. But when we found out that our fans could hear stuff they never would hear unless they traveled with us, we decided it could be a neat thing. It makes our fans part of the family.

And when they're knocking us for having the 900 line, they also don't mention that part of the money that line earns goes to United Cerebral Palsy, a charity for which our manager, Dick Scott, introduced us to and for whom we are the teen spokesmen.

They criticize us for talking to the audience too much during our shows. Well, we like working with the crowd. We enjoy that. I wouldn't mind if the critics were our fans, but usually they're not, and we don't perform for them. We are doing it the way we believe we should be doing it. We're doing it the best way we know how.

Jordan:

The teen magazines are really cool. They're very supportive of us. If it wasn't for the teen magazines, I don't think we'd have the success we've had. So I think we owe the magazines a lot. But people put us down for being in the teen magazines. And that's crazy—they're *teen* magazines, and we have teen appeal, so it makes perfect sense for us to be in them. There's nothin' wrong with it.

Other kinds of press—newspapers and some magazines—really

judge you before they've met you. It's like judging a book by its cover. They see we're young, they say we were created by a producer, and automatically they assume we're like puppets on a string. They don't give us credit for anything.

Some people have said we're talentless. That would hurt, except I know it's not true. Someday they'll know that, too.

Danny:

Our manager has explained to us that once you're on top, no matter who you are, some of the press just tries to knock you down. So we gotta understand that—and be happy that we're on top!

OUR REAL FRIENDS

Jordan:

When you're famous, you're suddenly all popular and stuff; you have friends you never knew you had poppin' out of the woodwork. Everyone's so nice to you and wants to do things for you, hang out with you. But a lot of these people are really phonies who wouldn't have given us the time of day a few years ago. We never really have trouble knowing who our friends are—that's not a problem for us.

Joe:

Aside from the guys in the group and our crew, I have only two close friends, Jonathan Schein and Paul Callahan. We grew up together and hung out at the monument in Jamaica Plain. It's big-time important for me that they are my best friends. They wouldn't even think of saying, "Why didn't you call me?" We have a real good understanding. They've come out on the road with me, so they know what I'm doing, and they've experienced all we go through.

When I go home, there are these people who come by. They're not really a gang, but a bunch of older guys that I used to look up to when I was a kid. They didn't bother with me then, but now they all have posters and stuff for me to sign. I'll sign them and be polite, but I know who my real friends are. You just laugh at the ones trying to be your friends.

Danny:

My closest friend is Tony Haley. He worked with me delivering airline tickets, way before we had any success. Now he's on the hype tip with me.

Jonathan:

We're each other's best friends, but we're together so much that it's good to get away and be with other friends. I've kept up with some of

TOP:
With UCP founder Jack Houseman during the 1990 Telethon (courtesy UCP)

MIDDLE:
Donnie with Florence Henderson at the United Cerebral Palsy Telethon (courtesy Alma Conroy)

BOTTOM:
Joe and friend Jon Schein with Jonathan and his mother in Florida (photo by Anne Woolf)

my old friends at home in Boston, but not all. Recently, I got a letter from my old high school teacher, and I started to cry, because I was just remembering the days when I was in her homeroom class. But you've kind of got to let those old memories go and move on.

I've made a lot of new friends on the road, especially during our first tour. We played Disneyworld a lot back then, a week's worth of shows. I met all these kids my age who worked there. I just sat down and started talking to this one kid, and he introduced me to his friends. We all went out to eat and stayed up all night talking. The next day we went swimming, shopping; it was cool. So I've kept in touch with these friends, and I see them whenever I'm in Florida.

The same thing happened with kids I met in Hawaii when I was there in December of 1988. I just got real close to a couple of people, and whenever I get the chance, I fly out to see them. When I met them, none of these people knew, or cared, that I was in a group; they just liked me for me.

GIRLFRIENDS

Joe:

This is the big thing everyone wants to know—do we have girlfriends? I think I speak for everyone when I say that we just don't have time for serious relationships. It's hard enough to meet people when you're on the road; it's impossible to get to know someone well enough to form a real relationship.

Jonathan:

Our other problem with girlfriends is that when people think you do have one, they get mad at the girl. Whenever it's printed that one of us has a girlfriend, the poor girl is in for it. When I appeared on the United Cerebral Palsy telethon with Tiffany, who's a very good friend, she got booed. She's a pro and she understands, so she wasn't hurt by it; but any other girl we might be going with could really get hurt. So in more ways than one, it's just easier for us not to have girlfriends right now. No promises about the future, though!

A B O V E :
With Elton John (© 1989 Larry Busacca)

O P P O S I T E :
At Madison Square Garden, New York (© 1989 Larry Busacca)

WHAT WE'RE REALLY LIKE

People are always curious about our personalities. We realize that it *is* hard to get to know us just by reading an article in a magazine, or even watching us up on stage for an hour or two. We hope you've gotten to know us a little better just reading this book. In this chapter, we're going to try and get a little closer. We're not gonna do that thing where we list our favorites and things like that, mainly because they're always changing. We can tell a magazine writer that we like the color red, but by the time it comes out, we can't stand that color anymore. So we're just gonna do our own thing, in no particular order, in our own words.

DANNY

Donnie calls me a perfectionist, but I don't know if I am. I just know that whatever I do, I want to do it right. When I work out in the gym, every set I do, I want to get the most out of it. It's true that I'm very into fitness. Here's the reason.

I think the whole thing started back in February 1989 when we were doing the video for "The Right Stuff." I was taking off my shirt one day, and I looked down and I had this, like, belly and I thought, "Uh-oh. Better get rid of this." So I started doing a lot of sit-ups, but I was doing them the wrong way and hurting my lower back. I was going to a gym and working out three times a week—except I didn't know what I was doing.

Luckily, in July, I met our bodyguard Butch—he joined us when we were doing the "Hangin' Tough" video—and he's a body builder. Butch really helped me and got me into shape. He taught me to do sit-ups the right way, which is more like crunches: you don't use your back, just curl up from the shoulders. He showed me how to use the Nautilus machines and free weights. We do our workouts together now, and we're real swift, so we work the heart at the same time. We'll go into a gym and do a whole leg routine, thighs, hamstrings, calves. We're so fast, everyone else will be sitting around doing their sets real slow, and we'll be gone and out of the gym. I try to go six days a week. So far, in seven months, I've gained seventeen pounds of muscle.

Just as I've found a way to exercise on the road, I've also found you can eat pretty healthy, even though I'm always on the go. It's not that hard. I have fruit all the time, and I'll have turkey instead of red meat. The meals we have are good, usually fish or vegetables.

But just feeling fit and taking care of myself, that's not the main reason this stuff means so much to me. I feel it's made me a better person. Because when you're working out every day, it's something to do, it keeps you busy and gives you peace of mind. And that makes you a nicer person toward everyone else.

Like I said, I'm self-disciplined. But it's funny, because there are certain things, like money, that I'm just not on top of at all. I have no idea

> **Donnie calls me a perfectionist, but I don't know if I am. I just know that whatever I do, I want to do it right.**
>
> —DANNY

how much I'm being paid for a concert. All I think about is that when I'm out there onstage, I want to do it right.

I can get crazy, but I don't let things get too far. I'll get in a water fight with the rest of the guys, but I'll only take it to a certain point. When I think things are getting out of hand, like if we're in a hotel and it's getting into the hallway, I'll just say, "That's it for me," and I'll quit, I'll just go to my room. But don't get me wrong, I love to have fun.

I always liked girls, and I always had a girlfriend, but there are times, even now, when I can get shy around girls. There was this one girl I really wanted to meet, but I was afraid I wouldn't be able to talk to her. She was so pretty, I felt too intimidated. So when I was going to meet her, I brought a friend along who's a real good talker. But this time it worked out; I was real chill, and I didn't need anyone to make conversation. I'd just thought I would.

Sometimes I like what I'm doing better than other times, but when you add it all up, my life is great.

JONATHAN

A lot of people say I'm shy, but I'm not shy. I'm just uncomfortable in certain situations; I never liked being in the spotlight.

I never liked being the center of attention, even when I was a kid. In school, I secretly wanted to be class president; I never wanted to be just another person there. But the thought of standing up in front of the whole class and speaking terrified me, so I never did it.

I guess it's kind of the same with the group in a lot of ways. I'm comfortable with someone else doing leads—though I have two on our *Step By Step* album—and I'm happy to be in the background. I'll never understand why girls go crazy over us. To me, I'm just *me,* no more special than anyone else.

I feel that way about all celebrities. I grew up listening to Elton John; I thought he was the greatest. I got the chance to meet him when he came to one of our shows in Los Angeles, and he was great; it was so cool to meet him. But he's just human. Everybody is just human.

I like quiet moments. I like to do solitary projects. When I was younger, I used to love to build doghouses and stuff. I completely did my room over. It's Art Deco. I went to this antiques dealer and got this old iron bed. It was so cool. But it was all rusty and nasty-looking when I brought it home. My mother thought I was crazy. But I just took sandpaper and sanded it down. Then I painted it glossy black, and I painted my walls white and, where the fireplace is, gray. Those are the kinds of things I like to do.

I love to be at home. I love to know things are being taken care of—

my fish tank, my bird cage, my bonsai trees. See, after my dad left, I was always the one helping my mother—not that I was the oldest, but that's just my personality—making sure repairs got done, the grass got cut. It worries me when I'm not home; those things are always on my mind. Last winter, we were on tour and there was some construction going on at the house, and I worried about that. Then my sister called and said we'd had a snowstorm and all the pipes burst. I really wanted to go home then! But the workmen there fixed everything up.

I'm a real animal lover. I have a little Shar-pei puppy that I take on tour with me. A lot of people think I'm crazy for having a dog out on the road, but the road is my home for months at a time. My puppy has his own bunk bed on our bus, and he sleeps with me in hotels. He's well trained. I trained him myself, personally. I miss him when I can't take him with me.

JORDAN

It's hard for me to describe myself, to say what kind of personality I have. If you think it's easy—try it! But here are a few things.

I'm not moody, I'm very laid back and easy to get along with. I can chill with anyone. I'm not a hilarious person, not the kind of guy who's gonna make you crack up and laugh, but I think I have a certain charm.

I definitely have a bad memory, and sometimes I can be very spacey. The other guys say I'm kind of lost in space. I guess that's because I'm thinking about my music a lot. Sometimes tunes will pop into my head and it takes a while to come down to earth again. But if you get my attention, you'll find I'm a great listener.

I don't take a compliment well. I just don't know how to take it; I get embarrassed. I would never do something like throw a party for myself. It's weird because I don't mind being in the spotlight when I'm onstage—I really love it—but when I'm with just a few people, or just *one* person, I can clam up. It's easier for me to talk to 15,000 people than just one. I don't know why. I have trouble expressing my thoughts in words. I can do it in music, but not with words.

Of course, if I know someone well, I'm okay. It takes me a while to warm up to people, so when I first meet someone new, I'm real quiet. When I get to know them well, then I let loose.

I've always been afraid of the supernatural, and still today I believe that there are ghosts and that there are powers we can't see and powers that are greater than what we do see.

I consider myself a spiritual person, but I don't really go to church regularly anymore. The message is the most important thing, and that's what I live by: love yourself, love God, and do good.

ABOVE:
Joe in the dressing room with Matthew, Jon and Jordan's nephew (courtesy Marlene Putman)

OPPOSITE:
Liftoff! (© 1989 Larry Busacca)

JOE

In certain ways I feel like a kid, because I've always been the youngest—with my family and with the group, too. But in other ways, I feel so much older than my age, older than the kids I grew up with. I've just experienced so much more. You can't help maturing when you're in a group like this and you're on the road so much.

I'm the one who's always ready to jump into any conversation, any fight, anything anyone's doing. I'm kind of physical; I like to wrestle and roughhouse with the guys. I think that's because I come from such a big, loving family, and we were always hugging and punching each other. Sometimes I just need to yell, to let out all this pent-up emotion. Just like my real family at home, the group and the crew are my family when we're on the road, and they understand. So it works out well.

I have a really good sense of humor. I think I'm funny, I'm always cracking jokes, and I appreciate a good laugh. I don't know exactly when I started to do this, but I can mimic anyone I meet. I do dead-on imitations of everyone in my family—it drives my mother nuts when she's telling a story, and I come in and retell it just the same way she said it—and everyone in the group too. It's fun for me, and it cracks everybody else up.

Right now, I'm into the show *The Simpsons*, 'cause I think it's the funniest thing on TV. I like comedies in the movies, too. When we're on the tour bus, I like watching funny movies, or playing Nintendo. Donnie and I spend a lot of time doing that.

There's another side to me, besides the fun-loving, carefree kid side. I'm pretty disciplined, and since I have to do my schoolwork every day—and I'm the only one in the group who does—that's cool. I have a tutor who travels with me, and I spend at least three hours a day with my head in the books. I'm going into my senior year, so I'm starting to prepare for the SATs.

I think I'm pretty perceptive about people. When I meet someone, I can size them up quickly and kind of get a handle on what they're all about. I like meeting and getting to know different kinds of people; I'm a good listener.

I'm not the most sensitive person. I hope I'm putting this right. I mean, I care a lot about other people, but if people make a joke about me or pick on me, I don't get hurt that easily. If I did, I never would have stayed in the group, 'cause they used to pick on me all the time. So I learned to have a thick skin.

Sometimes I can be real quiet, like I'll get into moods where I don't talk a lot, don't share my feelings and thoughts. But I like to surprise the people I love with other kinds of expressions. I did this one thing that really moved my mother. It was wintertime, and while she was in the house, I went outside and wrote in the snow in really large letters that took up the whole backyard: I Love You, Mom. That gave her a lot of pleasure, and me, too.

I do consider myself religious, and I have very strong family values. I think those are things about me that won't ever change.

DONNIE

I like to talk. Anyone who knows me or anyone who's ever interviewed me knows that. Usually, when the interviewer is finished, I'll just say, "Let's do more questions." Actually, more often it ends up being a conversation instead of an interview. I just really like to express myself, and I like to be sure that the person I'm talking to understands me, that I'm getting the information out correctly.

I always write. I always write my feelings. I write speeches sometimes. Sometimes I'll be on airplanes, and there'll be something on my mind. So, I'll take out those airsick bags and write on them. I have a whole collection of airsick bags at home with my feelings written on them. I have a lot of things at home; I never throw anything out. My room—well, I don't really have a room now, because we just moved and I haven't had a chance to unpack—is cluttered with stuff. I'm a saver; I save everything. My mother complains about it, but what she doesn't realize is that I get it from her.

There is a lot of junk in my room, but I always have rough ideas of where everything is. If I misplace something small, like a phone number, or my license, I might not know where it is exactly, but I know where to look. There are certain places where I just throw everything.

I like to take risks. I like livin' on the edge. I never learn my lesson, either. No matter what, when someone tells me, "Touch this and you're gonna get burned, you got burned every time you've touched it before, don't touch it," I'll still touch it. I don't like to be told not to do something.

It's the same way with girls. I get hurt, but I never learn my lesson. I could get hurt by a girl, but I'll still end up with the same girl, getting hurt by her again. Because I just live for the moment, I live on instincts, all the time.

I'm very sensitive. I've cried on stage sometimes. But I get frustrated. Nowadays, I might start to choke up and want to cry, but I usually have to get control of my emotions, because more than likely, I'll be called upon to say something. Just as the tears are about to plop out. I don't let it happen anymore. But I'm not ashamed to cry.

With me, what you see is what you get. I don't hide anything.

> " I like to take risks. I like livin' on the edge. I never learn my lesson either. No matter what, when someone tells me, 'Touch this and you're gonna get burned, you got burned every time you've touched it before,' I'll still touch it. I don't like to be told not to do something. "
>
> —DONNIE

DRUG-
FREE
SCHOOL
ZONE

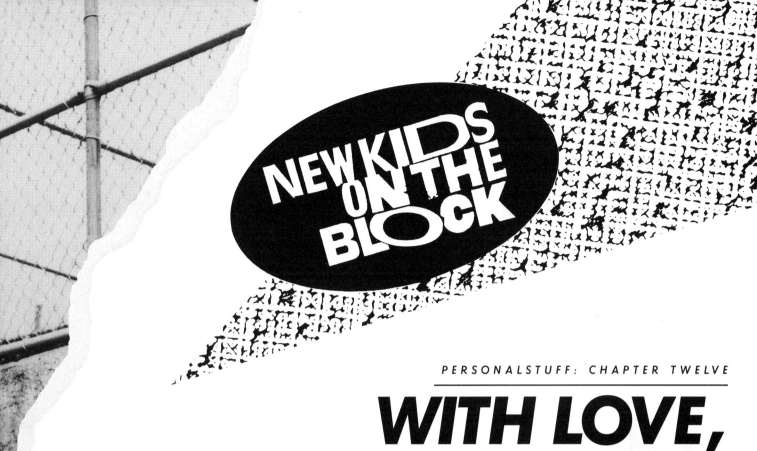

WITH LOVE, FROM US TO YOU

W e wrote this book so our fans could really get to know us, so *you* could feel the same way we do: that you are very much a part of our family. Before we sign off, though, there are a few thoughts we'd like to leave you with.

ON OUR IMAGE

We haven't tried to create any specific image, but we realize that we do have one. Different people think of us in different ways, but we hope that whatever our image is to you, it's a positive one. Someone once said that it's very hard to live up to your image, and we've discovered the grain of truth in that. We're not the squeaky-clean-cut boys some people have made us out to be, but we *are* good kids. We're not angels, but we're also not devils. We're just kids.

OUR MESSAGE

Donnie:

My message is one of hope, for our country, for our world, and for each and every one of us. I hope to see an end to the segregated mind-set we still collectively have. I hope to see an end to racial barriers. I hope that one day soon there will be no more black or white. I hope one day there doesn't have to be "black entertainment TV," because black people will be represented fairly on mainstream TV. I hope that in the music business, there won't be a separate black record chart and a pop record chart. Why does that have to be? If Bobby Brown has the number-one single on the black charts and it sells 500,000 copies, is it not a popular record because it hasn't "crossed over" to the [white] pop charts? I hope that singers like Bobby Brown and groups like us are starting to tear down the racial barriers.

I don't want to see black people and white people and Spanish people, Chinese people, Indian people, and Mexican people: I just want us to see ourselves and others as *people*.

Danny:

My message is simple, but I think it's been oversimplified in a way. "Say No to Drugs" has become a slogan that a lot of people use. When we say it, we really understand what that means. We've seen the damage that drugs can do—and we really understand how hard it can be for some people to say no. The neighborhoods we grew up in had a lot of drugs. Some of the people we grew up with—some of the people in some of our families—had drug problems. As teenagers, hanging out on the streets, we were offered drugs, too. And we made the choice to turn away, to say No. If we hadn't, we wouldn't be where we are today. We might not even be here at all.

Doing drugs leads you down a dead-end street; saying no opens up a whole wide world of options for you. It's *your* life to take in any direction *you* choose.

Jonathan:

There are so many issues concerning kids today that it can seem overwhelming. This may be the adults' world today—it's *our* world tomorrow. It's up to us to start thinking about it, to start cleaning up the environment and finding ways to end pollution.

The other message I have is not to give in to peer pressure. Whatever it is that other people are trying to talk you into, the final decision always comes down to you. It's your life. Just because someone else is doing something, that doesn't mean you have to. It's like the old saying: If so and so jumps off a bridge, does that mean you have to follow?

You've got to take control of your own life. If you blindly follow others, in the long run, it's gonna hurt you the most. And those other people you followed, when you need them, chances are they're gonna be long gone. You have to watch out for yourself.

Joe:

Stay in school. That may sound like an easy thing to say, but it's more important than you may know. No matter what you've got going today, or how smart you think you are, nothing lasts forever, and without an education, you're nowhere. A lot of people have asked me why I'm still working with a tutor, doing at least three hours of schoolwork a day—after all, I'm in a popular singing group, and my future seems assured. I don't think anyone's future is assured—we *all* need an education. No matter how tough the going gets in school, don't drop out: that little piece of paper that says you've graduated may come to mean a lot.

Jordan:

If you want to do something, keep at it, 'cause if you put your heart into it, you can do it. Remember, when I first started in the group, I had no leads, and that's what I wanted—to be a lead singer. I was frustrated, but I didn't quit; I just stuck it out doing back-ups until I got my chance. I feel that the best things come to those who wait. That's always been my motto.

Believe in yourself, have confidence in yourself, say no to drugs. Be the most understanding and loving person you can be. Be the best *you* can be.

FUTURESTUFF

As individuals and as a group, we've got a lot to look forward to. Here's some of it.

Jonathan:

I always want to stay in the music business, but in the future I'd like to get more into the behind-the-scenes stuff. That's what really turns me on. Right now, I'm learning every single aspect of this business, from how the crew operates on the road, to how our management operates in the big offices. I want to do it all—and I think I can.

On the personal side, I'm looking forward to buying my family a new home, with lots of yard and land so I can do things with it, take care of it. I'm a real nature freak. I want to have horses, just to be able to ride. And maybe a pond or something on the property. I want us all to live together, my whole family.

One day, of course, I see myself married—but not for at least a few years.

OPPOSITE TOP TO BOTTOM:
(© 1989 Larry Busacca)

Danny holding Daniela, his sister Melissa's baby (courtesy Betty Wood)

Florida, February 1990—Jonathan at the helm! (photo by Anne Woolf)

THIS PAGE TOP:
(© 1989 Larry Busacca)

THIS PAGE BOTTOM:
Jordan with Matthew, Thanksgiving 1989 (© 1989 Larry Busacca)

> **" If you want to do something, keep at it, 'cause if you put your heart into it, you can do it. "**
>
> **—JORDAN**

Joe:

I'm so young, I really feel like I do have my whole future ahead of me. Of course, I always want to be in the entertainment business. No question about it: that's what makes me happiest. But I also will take a break at some point to go to college full-time. I'm thinking about being a writer someday.

Down the road—way down the road—I would like to be married...with children. Yes, I would like a big family.

Danny:

My life is so great now, I mainly hope for more of the same. I want the group to go on forever, even when we're "Old Dudes On The Block." I've found I love being in the studio, and I think I have a talent for engineering, producing, and writing music too. That's the direction I'd like to expand into creatively.

I'm looking forward to moving into my own apartment—which will be in the converted attic of my family's home. For the immediate future, anyway, I don't see my family enough to want to move out. And one day for myself, of course, I plan on settling down with an incredible girl, getting married, and raising a bunch of kids, pretty much the same way I was raised, with love.

Donnie:

I have so many racing thoughts, that I just want to sit down with my thoughts and take care of them. I'd like to find the time to do that. But I'm gonna do a lot more music—New Kids music and other music too. I want to do music that's challenging and fun.

My little brother's starting to get his music going, and I'm very involved with him. That's gonna be my favorite. He's a rapper, and we're callin' him Marky Mark & The Funky Bunch. He's got a band, a deejay, and two dancers, and Mary Alford and I are helping put it all together. We're called Cheezy-Lou Productions.

I'm also working with another rap group, The Northside Posse. They're really good—I know these guys from high school—and I'm just helping to put the finishing touches on their stuff and get that music out there.

Jordan:

I see the group still making records, putting out great songs, and I think we're only gonna get better. I'm a person who looks at everything and tries to learn from all of it. I don't see myself as some big superstar who knows it all. I'll always be learning something new. That's how I've always been and I think how I'll always be. That way, I'll become better at what I do. I'll definitely stay in the music industry. Even if New Kids ends, I'll still want to do solo stuff. I hope I'll always be an entertainer, and a writer and producer as well.

I've always seen myself as married and having a kid, but I can't see doing that and being real active in this business at the same time. They both take a full commitment, and I don't think it would be right to have a kid and then go off on the road or something. I feel if I do get married, I should give 100 percent of my energy to my family and my marriage.

NEW KIDS ON THE BLOCK: DOWN THE ROAD

New albums

are always gonna be in our future, we hope. There's so much to say musically, and as the years go on, we'll be having more and more input into our releases. We've already started to write songs; we're already doing some of the producing. Soon, we hope to be playing instruments on our records, too. Mainly, we're looking forward to putting out the hypest grooves in the music biz!

New concerts

are always just around the corner. We love performing and don't want to ever stop. We love bringing our music to you in all corners of the world; we love getting to meet our fans. As long as you want to see us, we're on our way!

Our cartoon show

is our first TV series, and we're convinced it's gonna be really cool. Our animated characters are just like us, and they'll be getting into all sorts of adventures. Each episode will end with a cliffhanger—*and* some live action footage of us in concert.

Our movie

is still on the drawing board as we write this, but there's nothing we're looking forward to more. We've signed a contract with Columbia Pictures. We want it to be real, we want it to be a good story, and we want it to have the hypest soundtrack in the 1990s!

WITH LOVE, FROM US TO YOU

We'll never stop being the "hardest-working Kids in show biz," and (to borrow our own phrase) we really and truly will be Lovin' You Forever. Thanks for everything, from the bottom of our hearts.

THIS PAGE TOP:
Joe and Jonathan with Matthew (courtesy Marlene Putman)

THIS PAGE BOTTOM:
(© 1990 Larry Busacca)

OPPOSITE:
(© 1989 Larry Busacca)

(© 1990 Larry Busacca)